Flatpicking Celtic

Arranged and Fingered by Allan Alexander

Other books and recordings in this series:

Flatpicking Medieval Guitar
Folksongs for Guitar from Near and Far
A Bouquet of Waltzes for Guitar
JS Bach Partita BWV 997
Eight Concert Rags by Scott Joplin
The Essential Greensleeves
The Balkan Book for Guitar
Mostly Medieval Music for Guitar
Celtic Music for Guitar Vols I & II
Renaissance Music for Guitar Vols I & II
Music of Spain and South America for Guitar
The Spanish Collection
Music of the British Isles
Flamenco Music for Guitar
World Music for Guitar
15 Venezuelan Waltzes for Guitar
12 Rhythmic Dances for Guitar
8 Scarlatti Sonatas for Guitar
The Guitarist's Lute Book
Easy Pieces for Guitar
Christmas Music for Guitar
Balkan Music for Mandolin
Medieval Music for Mandolin Vol I & II
Mandolin Music for Medieval Faires
Mandolin Music for Renaissance Faires
Airs of the Scottish Renaissance for Mandolin
Renaissance Music for Mandolin
Music of Spain & South America for Mandolin
Traditional Dances of Spain and South America for Mandolin
Early Dance Music for Mandolin
Celtic Music for Mandolin
Christmas Music for Mandolin
31 Pieces for Renaissance Lute
Easy Pieces for Lute
A Variety of Music for Renaissance Lute
The Christmas Lute
The Celtic Collection for Piano
Celtic Music for Flute & Guitar
Renaissance Music for Flute & Guitar
Ancient Airs, Cantigas & Dances

Published by exclusively by ADG Productions
15517 Cordary Avenue • Lawndale, CA 90260
ISBN 1-934163-27-9
web site address: www.adgproductions.com • e-mail: adgordon@adgproductions.com
Copyright © 2010 ADG Productions
No part of this book may be reproduced or transmitted in any form, electronic or mechanical without permission in writing from the copyright holder.
Printed in Canada

Attn: All customers
The audio mp3 files are available
to download for free at:
www.digitalsheetmusicdownloads.com/audio-files.html
Password: dsmdaf1953

Flatpicking Celtic Guitar

Music Copyright © 2010 Allan Alexander
All Rights Reserved

Printed in the Canada

Flatpicking Celtic Guitar

1. Man of the House • Aleksandra found this piece and I liked it immediately. I has everything a great Celtic piece needs. The low D in the piece gives a great powerful pedal for your own accompaniment. In all of these pieces, see how often you can leave your left hand fingers down. It will make the pieces easier to play and the ringing notes will make a nice harmony.
2. Thomas Leixlip the Proud • Turlough O'Carolan is my absolute favorite composer of Irish music. His melodies and phrasing show a great deal of originality. He is the greatest Irish composer that I know of, and he is also considered an National Irish treasure. He lived in the Baroque period which was 1650 to 1750.
3. I Serve a Worthie Ladie • This piece is from a wonderful collection of music from Scotland called "The Skene Manuscript." It is a collection of music from Scotland with a very distinct sound. The collection was for Mandora, which was a small pear shaped instrument from the lute family. The collection is all in Tablature, and the instrument had four pairs of strings. This piece is one of my favorite from the collection.
4. I Choys to Ly My Lon • From the Wemyss Lute Book (c. 1644-1648)
5. Hewlett • This is another piece by the wonderful Turlough O'Carolan. It's a lush, melodious, lovely piece by the master of Irish harp music. O'Carolan was a blacksmith's apprentice until he contracted smallpox at the age of eighteen and the disease left him blind. In Ireland at this time, when someone was born blind, they became a musician. He learned the harp and set off to perform for patrons.
6. Little Beggarman • I first heard this performed by Ian and Sylvia. I loved the piece and the way they did it. Here, I just do it without any accompaniment notes; it's just a great melody which can stand on its own.
7. Garrett Barry • The music in this book is a mixture of old manuscripts for lute and mandora and also traditional Irish music. Garrett Barry is a traditional piece and quite a bit of fun to play.
8. The Fisherman's Lilt • There are some interesting surprises in the phrasing of this piece. So often the phrases of a traditional piece are predictable, and to compensate, the arranger will try and make the harmony or variations interesting. The phrasing is so important anad whoever composed this piece knew this and took advantage of it.
9. Eleanor Plunkett • As you can tell, I really like the music of O'Carolan. Here is another wonderful example. And to continue my story about him. When he played for patrons, he didn't do all that well because the other harpers had started when they were very little. One kind patron took him aside and explained that he needed something else to make him unique, and he suggested that he compose, and compose he did. He wrote at least two hundred and fourteen pieces!
10. Dermott O'Doud • It's easy to overlook many of the tunes of Carolan because they are so short. This one was so beautiful that I wanted to hear more, and I wrote a variation for it. If you like the tune, you might try writing a variation for it yourself.
11. Cremonea • To me, Dermott O'Doud, Cremona and the Queen's Dream all have a similar type of melancholy sound. Before I wrote the variations I would group them together but now with the variations, they can be played individually. Each one is a jewel. Be sure to let the notes ring as long as possible, keep those bass notes down, let others ring as long as possible as long as they are not dissonant.
12. Song of the Chanter • What is it about some pieces which are so attractive, so appealing that you like them right away and you keep liking them year after year. The Song of the Chanter is one of those pieces for me. It caught me right away and just keeps catching me. It's a traditional piece with no apparent composer. Jessica Walsh helped me with the variation.
13. A Toy • This is a short lute piece from Jane Pickering's Lute book. It's only eight measures with an additional eight measures of variation. A "Toy" in a lute book was something that you played with. A piece which was usually short where the player added the variations. I added many to this tune as they just seemed to write themselves. Try writing some yourself, you might be surprised at the results.
14. Separation of Soul and Body • Separation of Soul and Body - A haunting melody is such a friend sometimes. Late at night, the snow or rain falling... warm inside, playing "Separation" over and over again. I love this tune. This tune really shows you how a great tune, though it is short, can be incredibly effective. It's one of my favorite Carolan tunes. When I perform it, I do each section 2 times, then repeat the entire piece.

15. Lilt Milne • This is another piece from the Wemyss Lute book which is from Scotland. It has a nice dreamy feel to it. Anytime you have notes ringing it's going to fill out the overall harmony of the piece.
16. Wo Betyd Thy waerie Bodie • This is a lute piece from the Straloch Manuscript. It's only eight measures long but it's such a nice tune. I added a few variations to it. The notes you will be playing in the first eight measures are the same notes, except a minor third below, that the lute played. Let the notes ring.
17. Carolan's Welcome Home • At the beginning of his career Turlough O'Carolan was not very highly regarded as a player because he started so late in life. If it wasn't for his composing, no one would know of him today.
18. Star of the County Down • Some of the Lyrics to this beautiful piece are: Near to Banbridge Town, in the County Down One morning in July, Down a boreen green came a sweet colleen, And she smiled as she passed me by; Oh, she looked so neat from her two white feet To the sheen of her nut-brown hair, Sure the coaxing elf, I'd to shake myself To make sure I was standing there. As she onward sped I shook my head And I gazed with a feeling quare, And I said, says I, to a passer-by, "Who's the maid with the nut-brown hair?" Oh, he smiled at me, and with pride says he, "That's the gem of Ireland's crown, She's young Rosie McCann from the banks of the Bann, She's the Star of the County Down.
19. Sheebeg Sheemore • Back to our story about O'Carolan's composing. One of the first places he visited was the home of George Reynolds, and hearing that his playing had much to be desired, he suggested he needed something extra and suggested he start composing. That night O'Carolan wrote his first piece which is the famous "Sheebeg Sheemore." Mr Reynolds liked it and encouraged him further.
20. The Queen's Dream • This is a lovely piece suitable for any gig. If you are a tablature reader, consider taking some time to learn how to read notation. You will find a lot of information which is not in tablature. It will give you another perspective on music. It's great mental exercise in the beginning and something that you will be glad you did for the rest of your life.
21. Nyth Gwcw • This is a piece I loved the first time I head it. The title means "The Cuckoo." It's one of the harder pieces in the book so give it time to get better. It will take longer to learn than you think, but you will be able to play it better than you imagine if you stick with it.
22. Lady Laudian's Lilt • Rory Dall - An early lute piece from the Straloch Manuscript. The first part is almost the original; the variation is a pleasant contrast. It's another one of my favorites.
23. Fanny Power • Written by Turlough O'Carolan for Elizabeth Power who was an heiress, daughter of David and Elizabeth Power. Fanny Power was married Richard Trench. It's a nice tune and can also be played a lot slower than I chose to do for this recording.

Notes to the Musician

Playing with a plectrum or pick creates different problems for an arranger than would creating music for a finger-style player. The most obvious problem is that with a pick, you cannot play two notes at the same time unless they are on adjacent strings. So as an arranger, I can't choose a bass note on the sixth string and a treble note on the second string and expect you to play it with a pick. Generally, we have to play all the notes in between. This limits an arranger, and a piece for classical guitar, or fingerstyle guitar is going to look a lot different than one for flatpicking. This doesn't mean we can't still do a great arrangement, only that it going to be different.

Part of doing a great arrangement is always taking advantage of the strengths of an particular instrument. I remember when I was first doing arranging for the flute and realized that it could sustain notes in a way the guitar can't. You can do some beautiful things with those sustained notes. The steel string guitar has some wonderful ringing sounds, and I try to take advantage of them in the arrangements, but I need your help to make the pieces sound that way. Keep your fingers down even when the music doesn't indicate it, the piece will sound so much better. Be sure to keep your fingers on those bass notes and let them ring for as long as you can as long as they aren't dissonant.

Early music notation was very basic. It was devised so that the clergy could write down hymn melodies. There is a collection of music titled "The Cantigas of Santa Maria" which was published in the thirteenth century. It is a collection of over four hundred songs in praise of Virgin Mary. The notation was very basic and when secular music grew, the notation was not sophisticated enough to enable music for the lute or keyboard as it became more complex. So the lute went to a tablature system. It was very much like guitar tablature today, except in most cases, there were letters instead of numbers. Lutenists still use this system today, and there is very little music a lutenist would be interested in which is not in tablature.

The one problem with tablature is that although it will tell you when a note starts, it does not tell you how long the note should be sustained. John Dowland, who was very famous lutenist of the times, gave specific instructions about how to sustain notes while playing tablature. I won't quote him here, but this is the crux of what he says. Keep your fingers down while playing. If you are playing notes in a middle voice, keep the fingers down which are holding the treble notes and the bass notes. If you do run out of fingers and you must lift them, in most cases, lift the fingers which are holding down the treble notes and continue to hold the bass.

In this collection, it is a very good idea to hold the fingers down almost anytime you can. Keep your fingers down. When you do this, the melody you just played will become the harmony for the forthcoming notes.

Other things to keep in mind with this music is that much of it was dance music, so play rhythmically. A metronome is a handy way to make sure that you are not going to stray. You can also play with other people which can also keep you steady. Early instrumental music was often played in unison. These pieces present a perfect opportunity to come together with other musicians you might know and play music.

The music is presented in both notation and tablature. If you don't read, this is a perfect collection to begin to become familiar with notation. It will open up an entire world to you if you are able to read music.

I wish to give special thanks to Ian McConnell who has recorded this edition on a small body parlor guitar. I think he has done a terrific job. I hope you will enjoy the recording and also enjoy playing the music in this collection. Allan Alexander lives with his lovely wife Aleksandra in Tucson, AZ.

Allan Alexander

Traditional Celtic

6th to D

Man of the House

Arrangment and Variations
by Allan Alexander

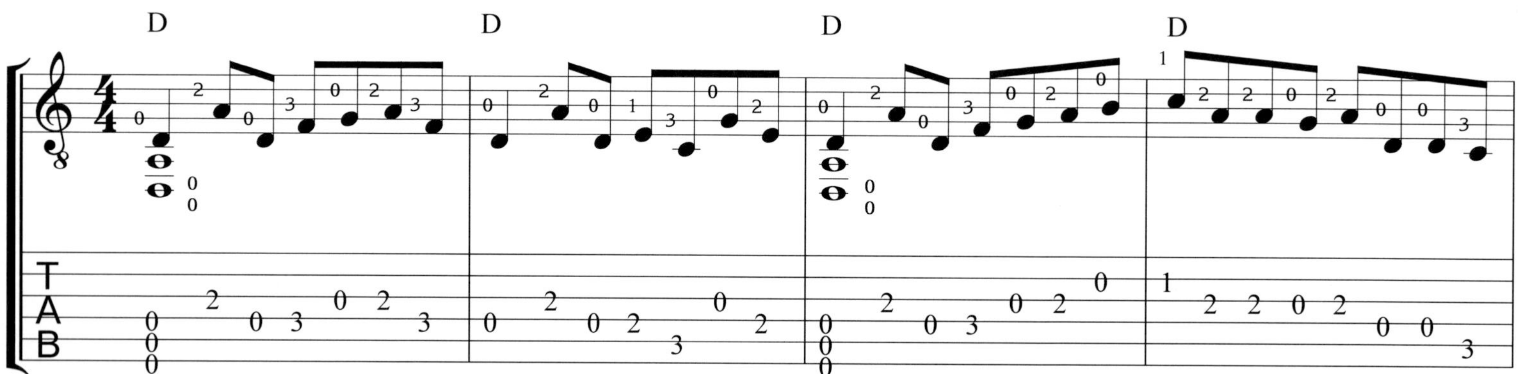

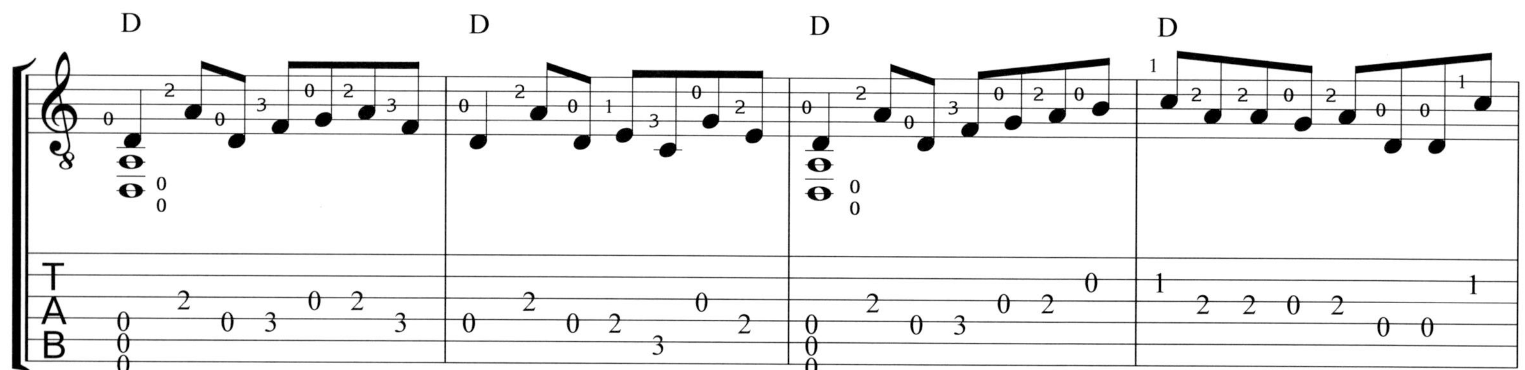

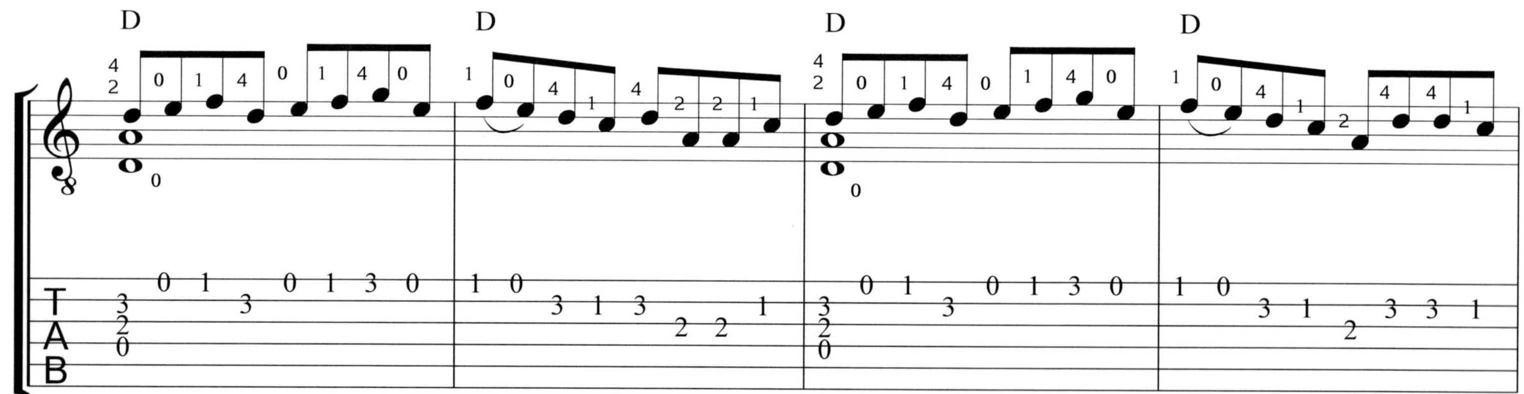

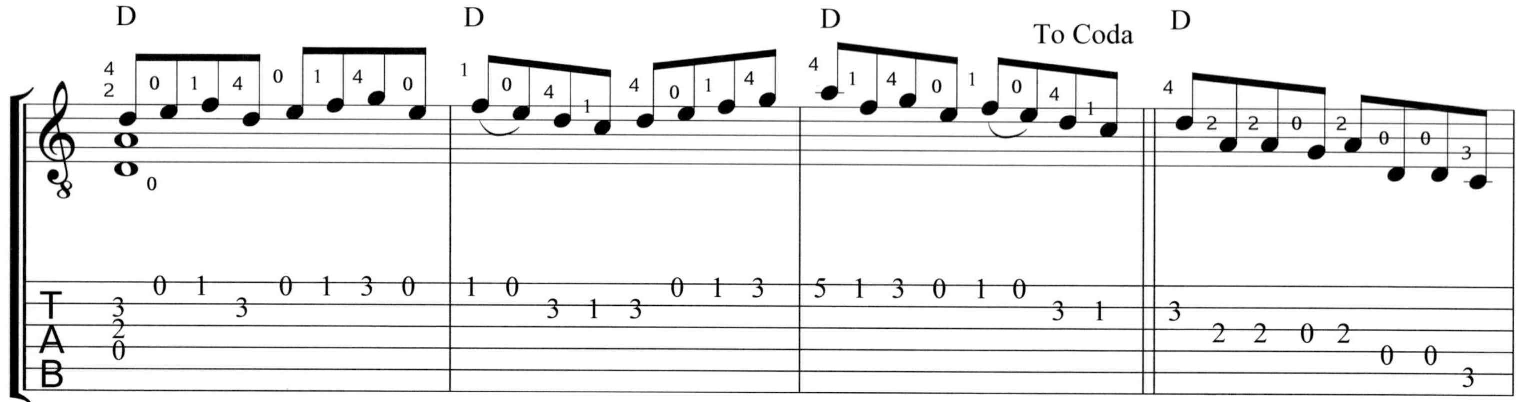

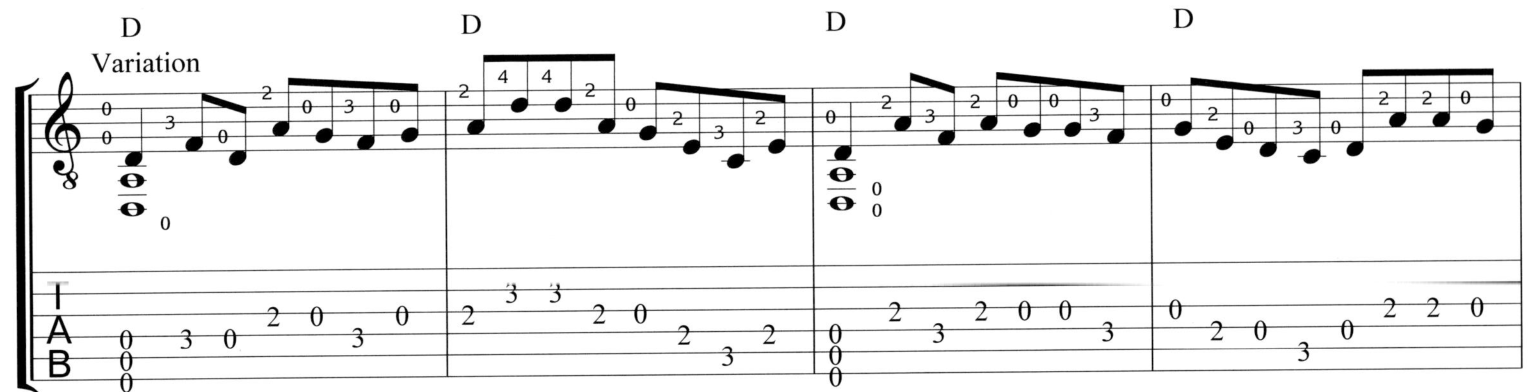
D
Variation
D
D
D

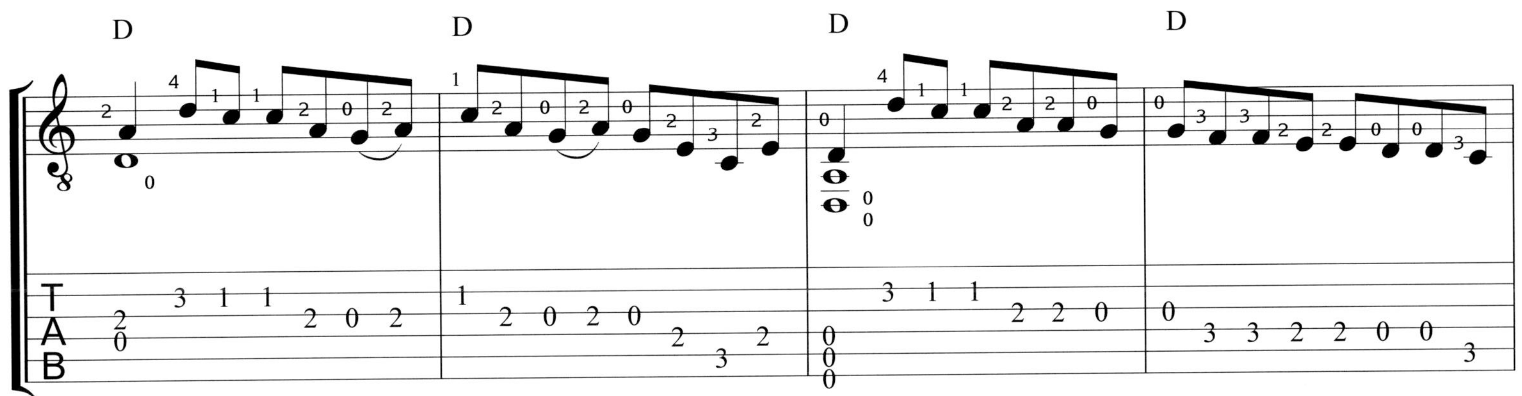
D
D
D
D

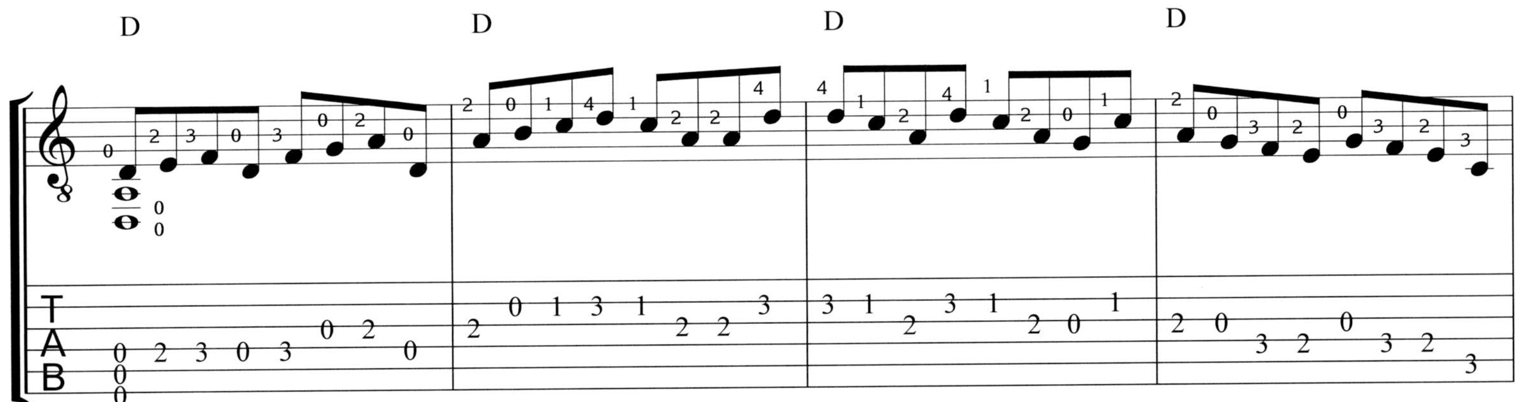
D
D
D
D

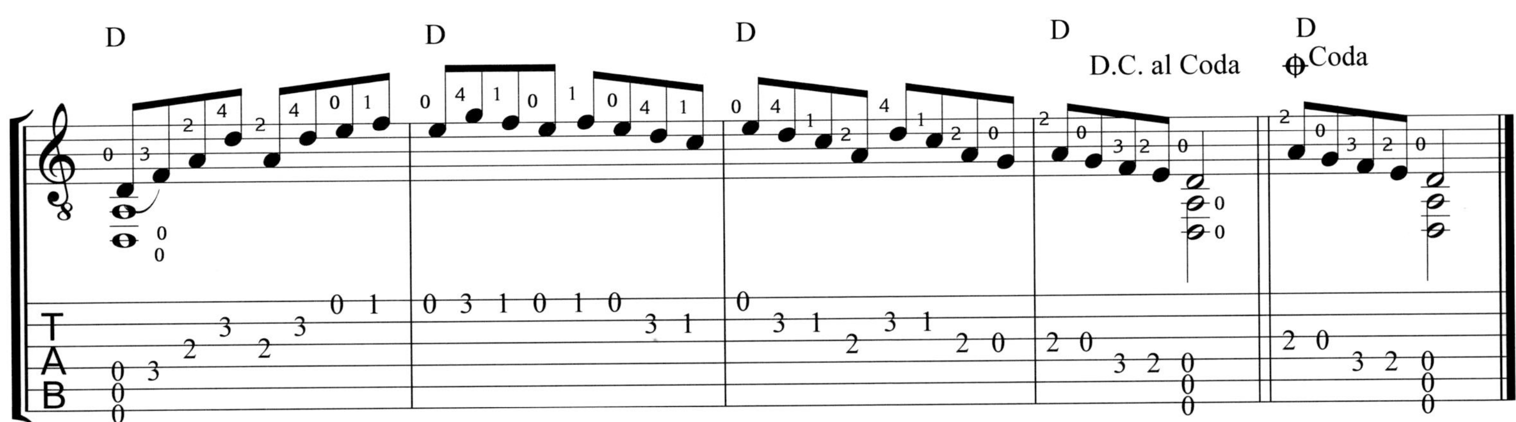
D
D
D
D
D.C. al Coda
D
Coda

Turlough Carolan

Thomas Leixlip the Proud

Arrangement and Variations
Allan Alexander

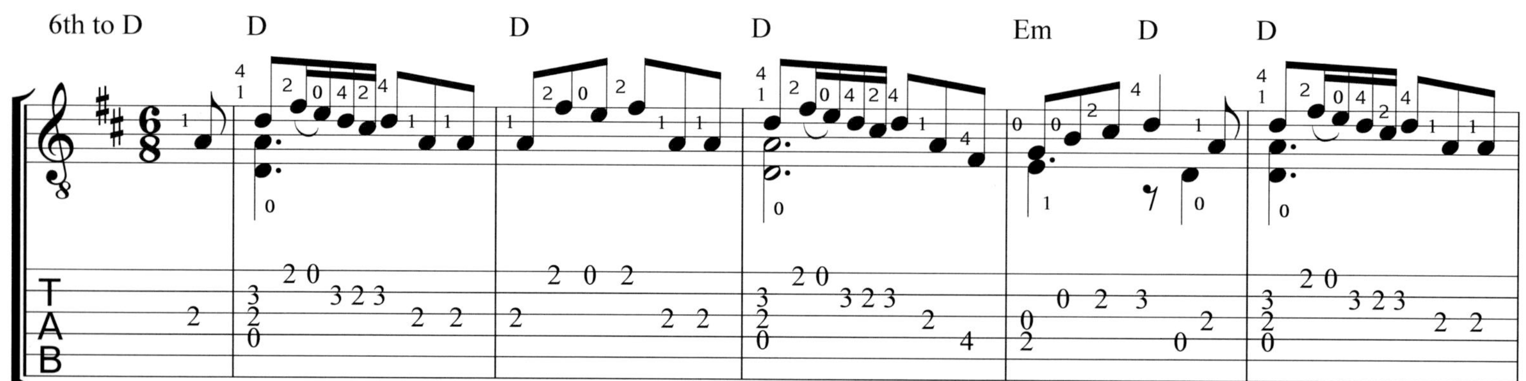

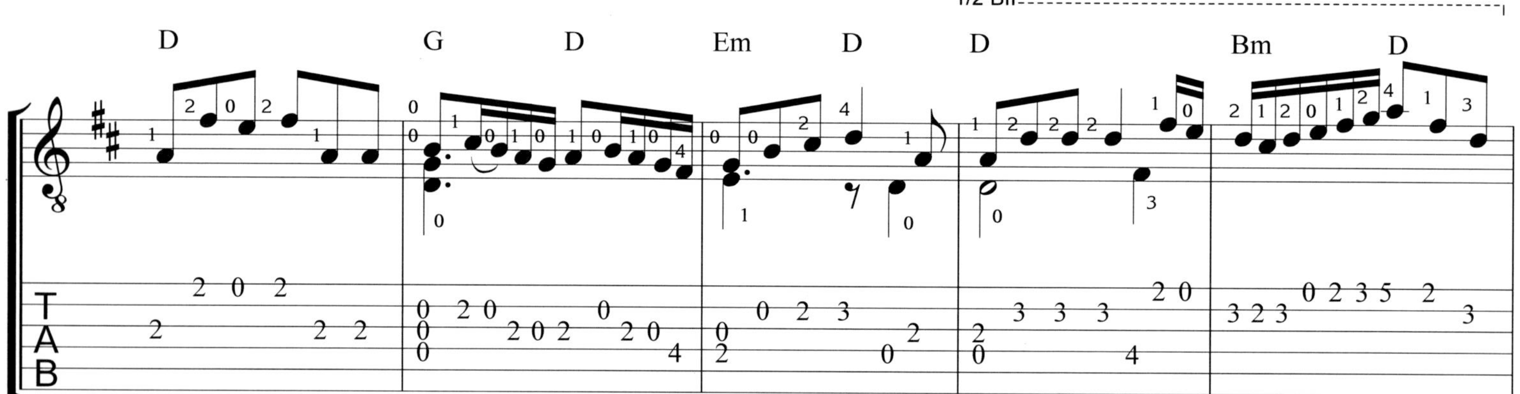

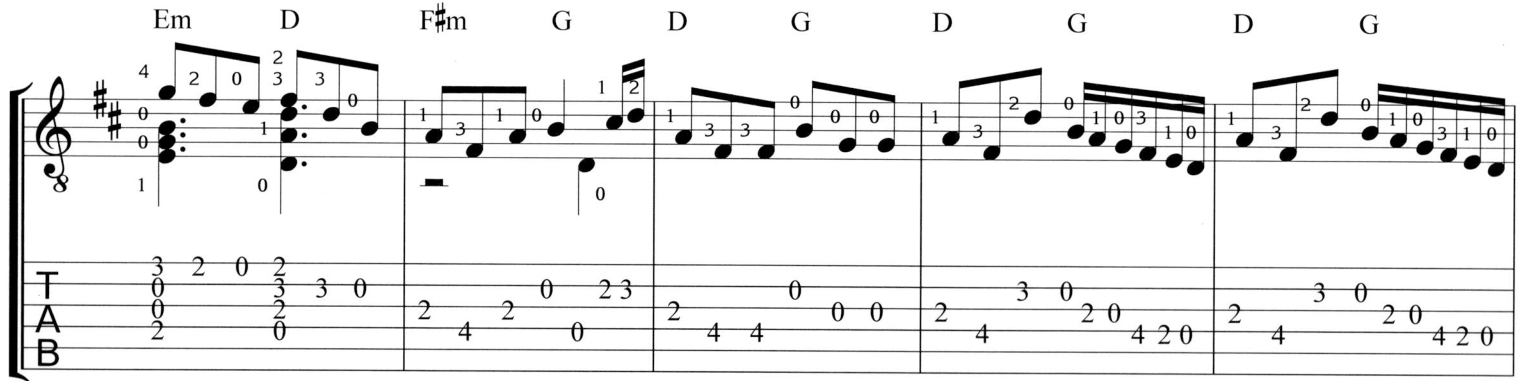

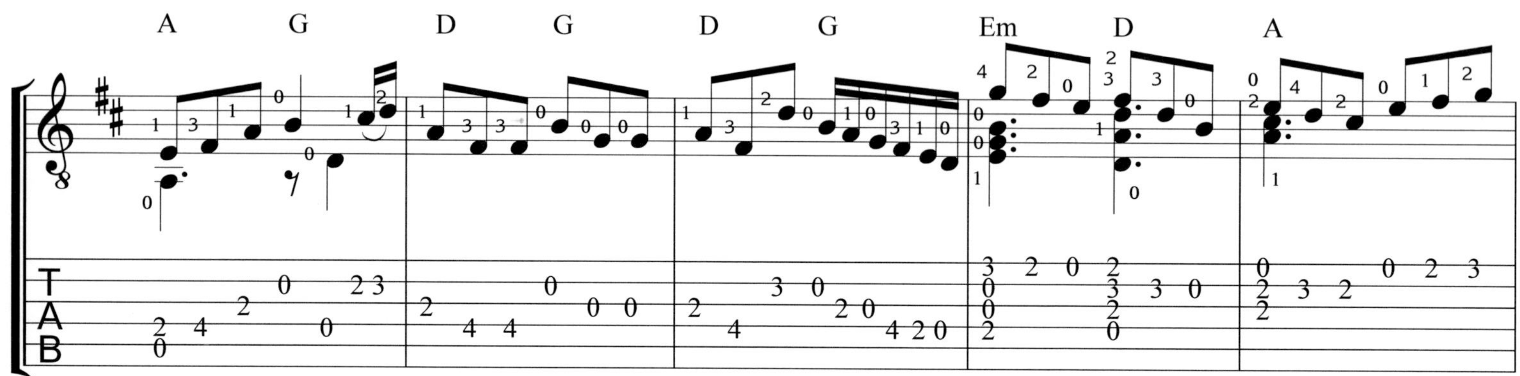

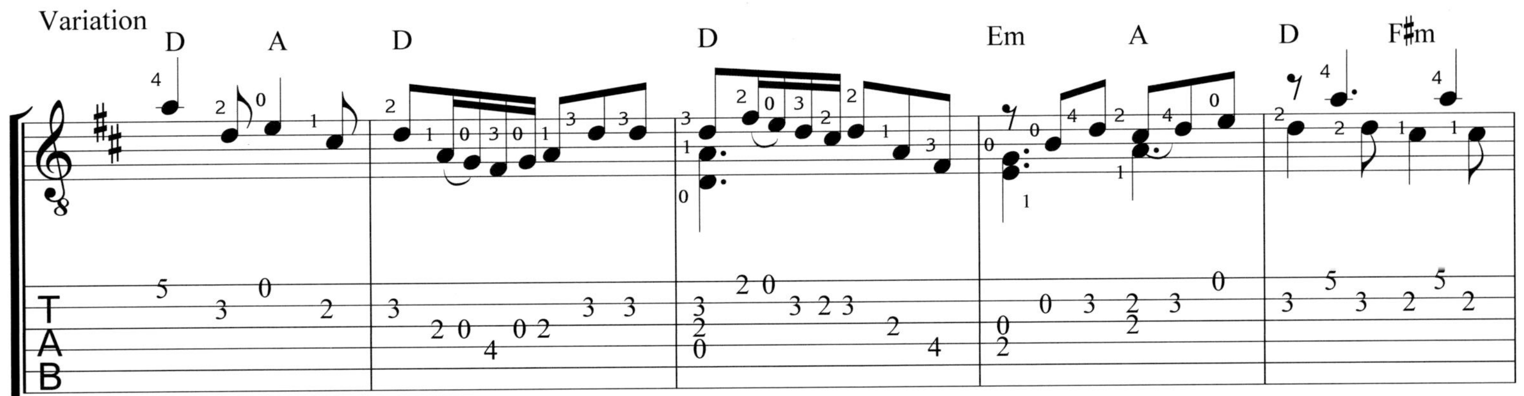
Variation
D A D D Em A D F♯m
TAB

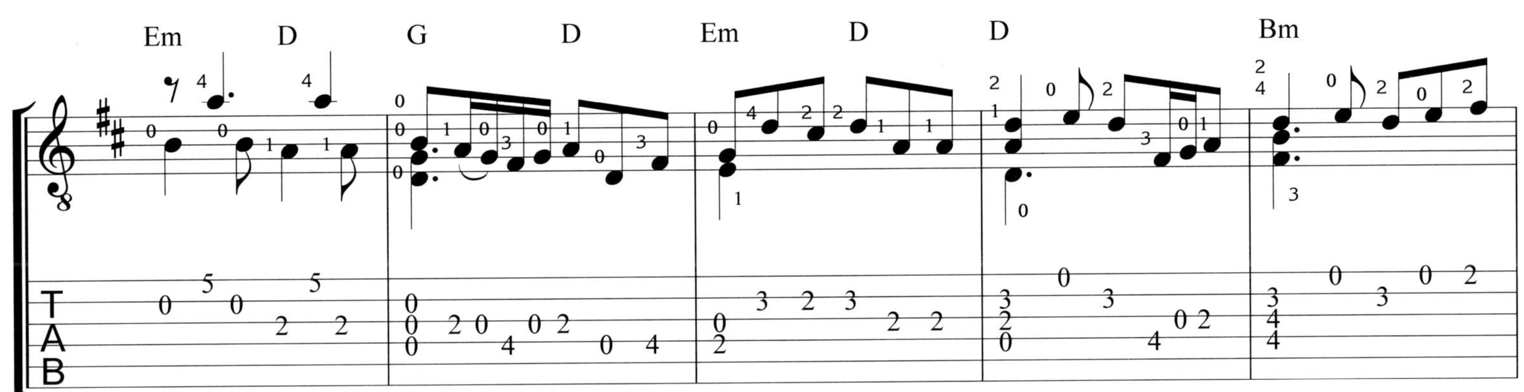
Em D G D Em D D Bm
TAB

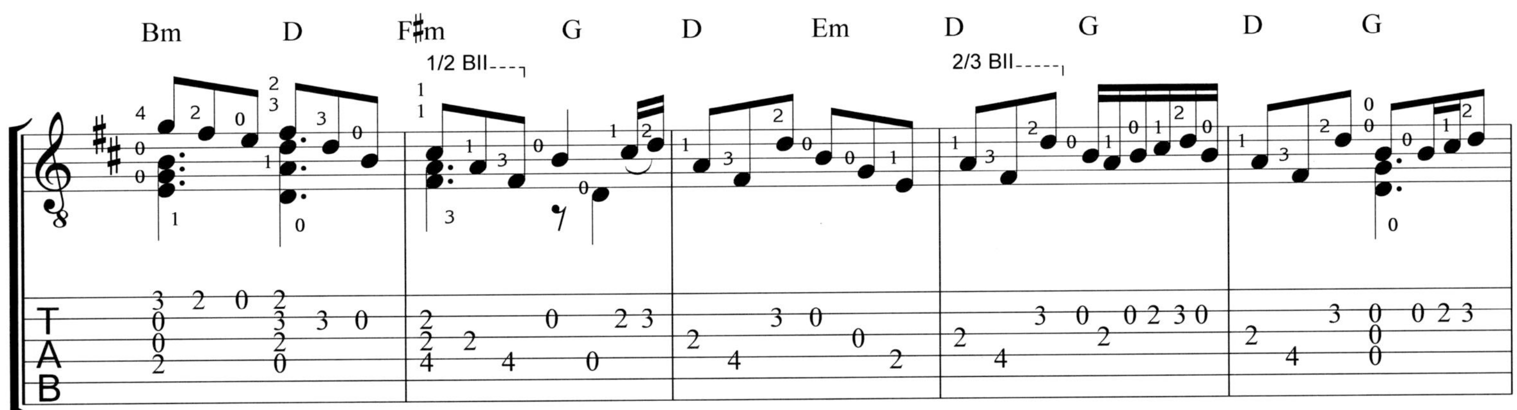
Bm D F♯m G D Em D G D G
1/2 BII
2/3 BII
TAB

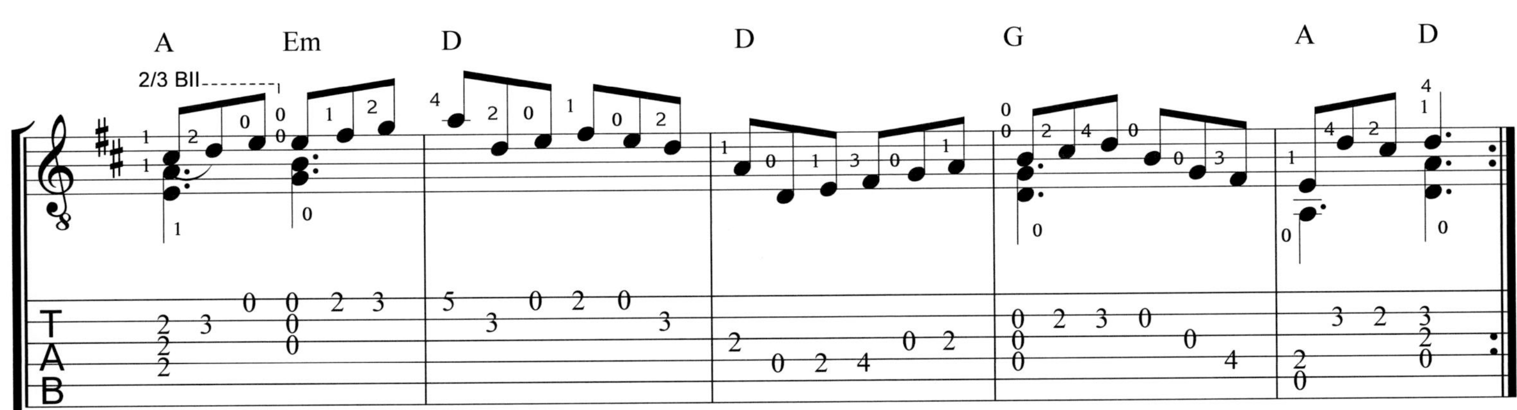
A Em D D G A D
2/3 BII
TAB

I Serve a Worthy Ladie

From the Skene Manuscript

Arrangement by
Allan Alexander

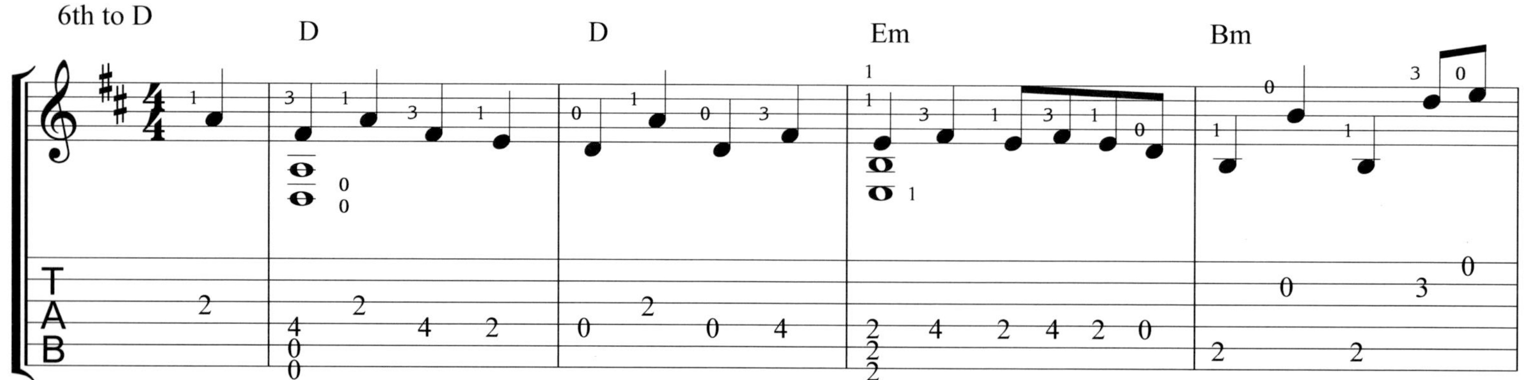

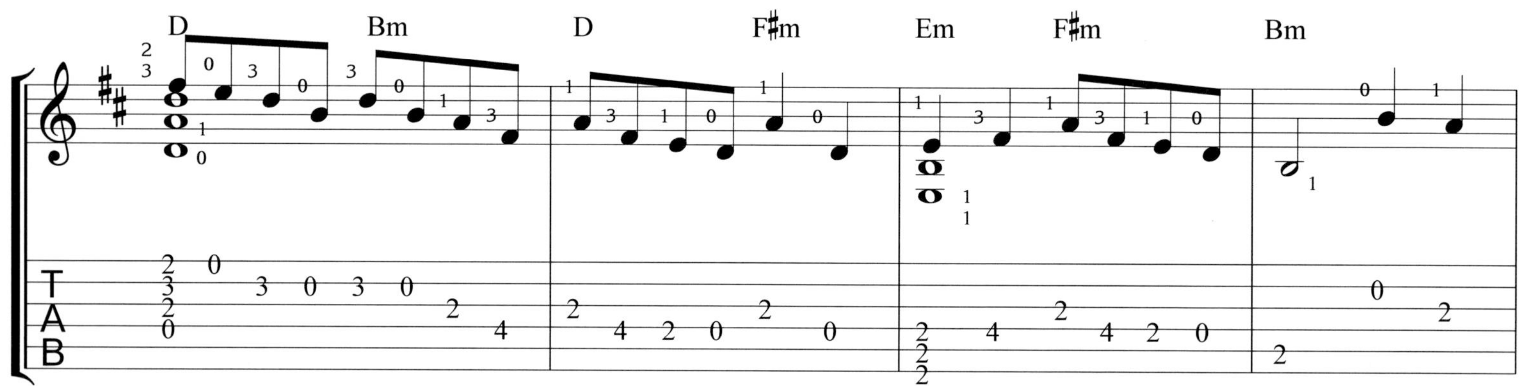

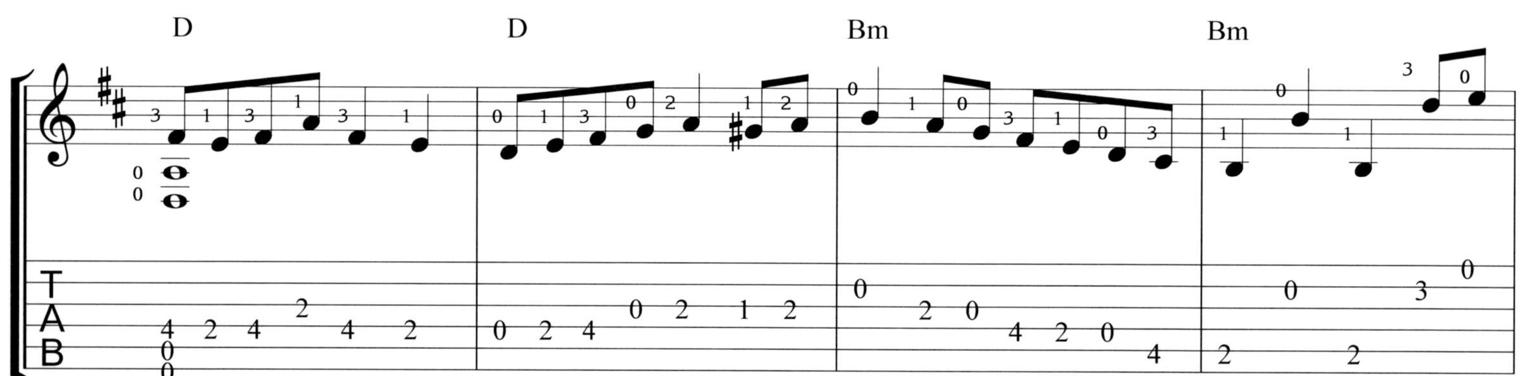

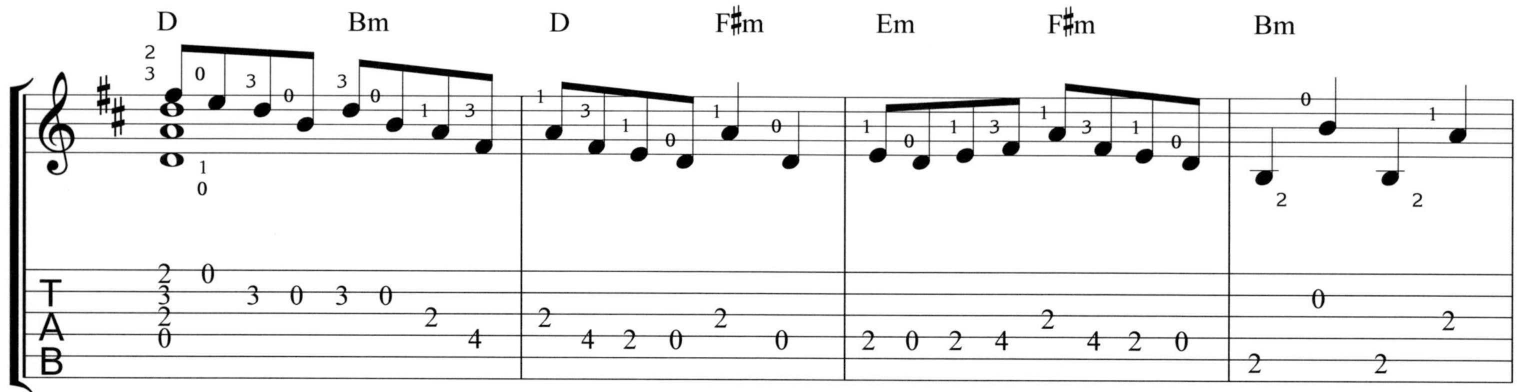

D
D
Em
Bm
D
Bm
F♯m
Bm
Em
F♯m
Bm
D
A
D
F♯m
Em
G
Bm
D
Bm
D
F♯m
Em
F♯m
Bm
T
A
B

I Choys to Ly My Lon

From the Wemyss Lute Book

Arrangment and Variations
by Allan Alexander

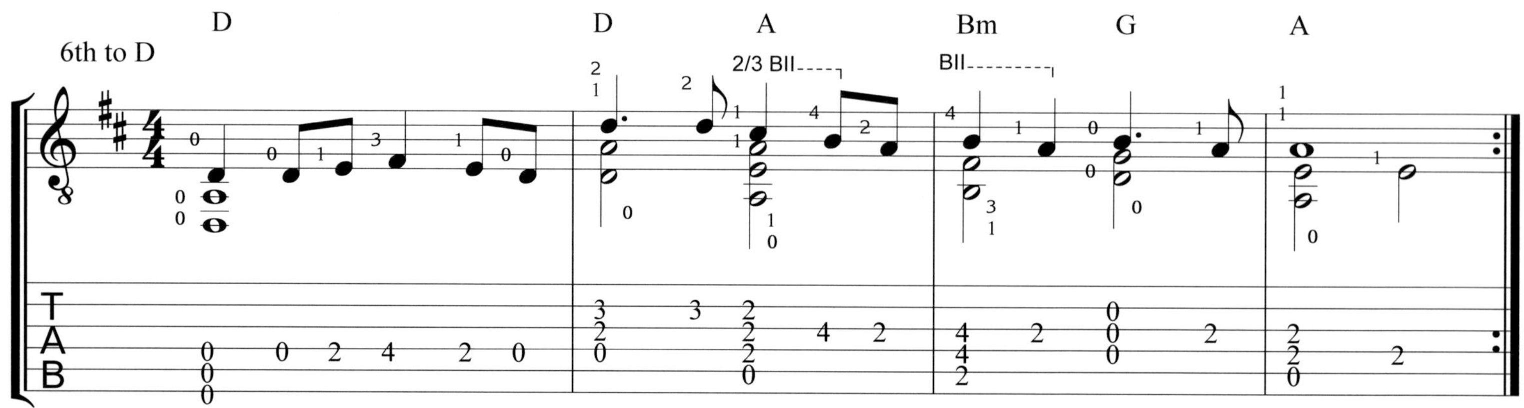

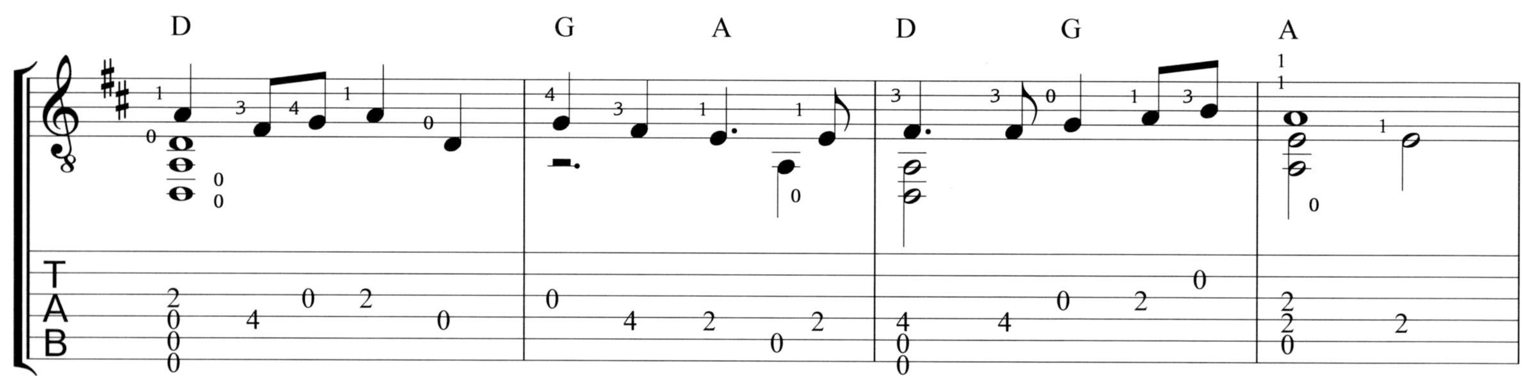

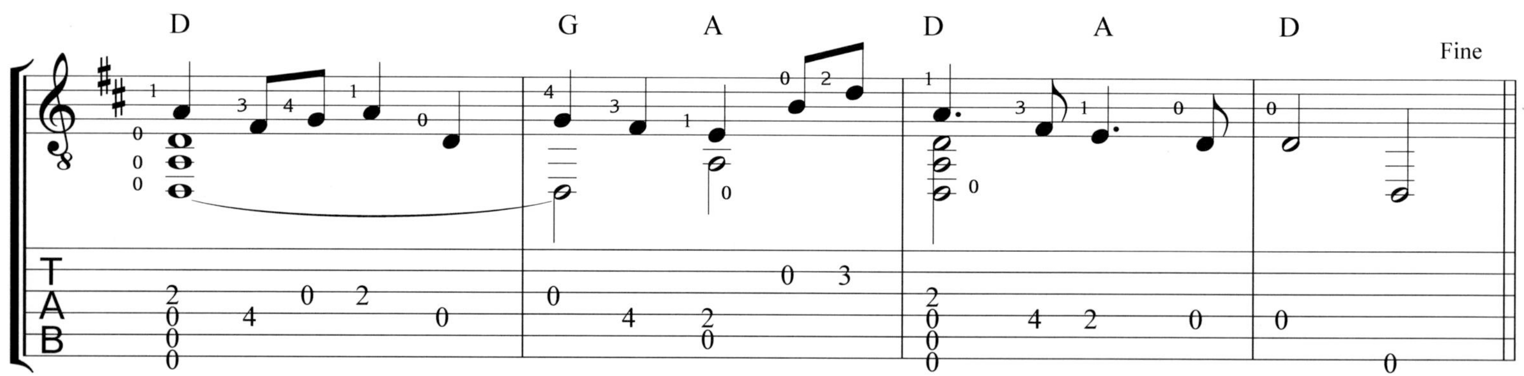

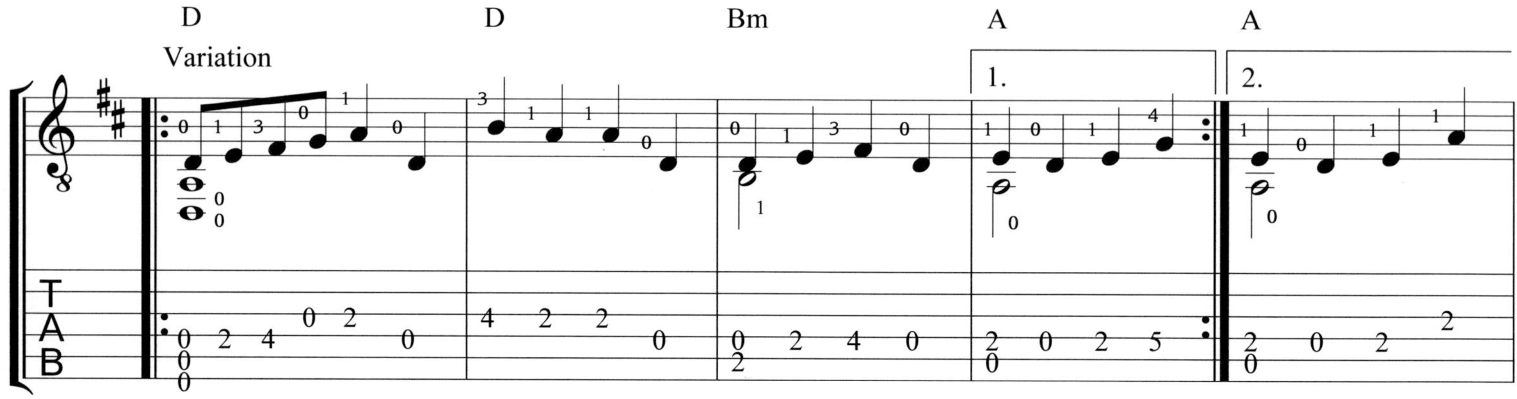

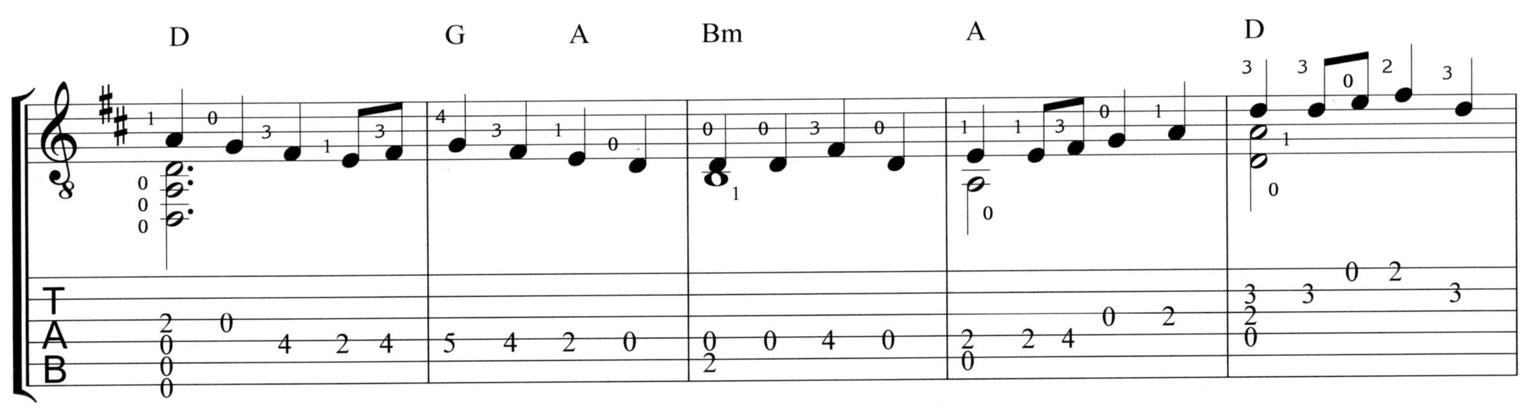
D
G
A
Bm
A
D
T
A
B

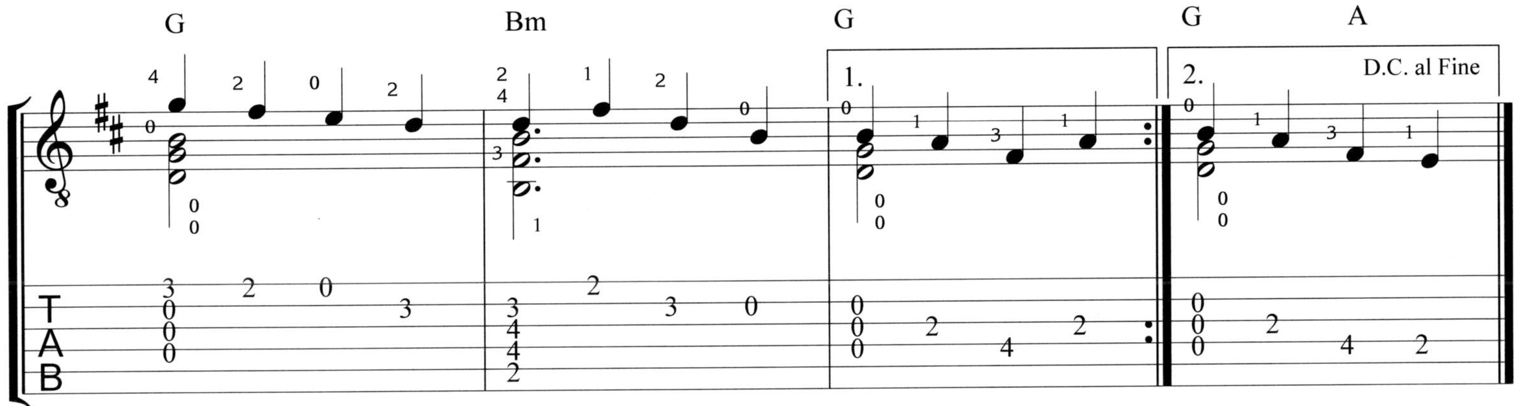
G
Bm
G
1.
G
A
2.
D.C. al Fine
T
A
B

Turlough Carolan
Hewlett
Arrangement & Variations by
Allan Alexander
6th to D
2/3 BII
5/6 BIII
BII

D
A
D
Bm7
D
Em
D
D
Variations
D
A
Bm
G
D
Em
D
D
D
A
Bm
G

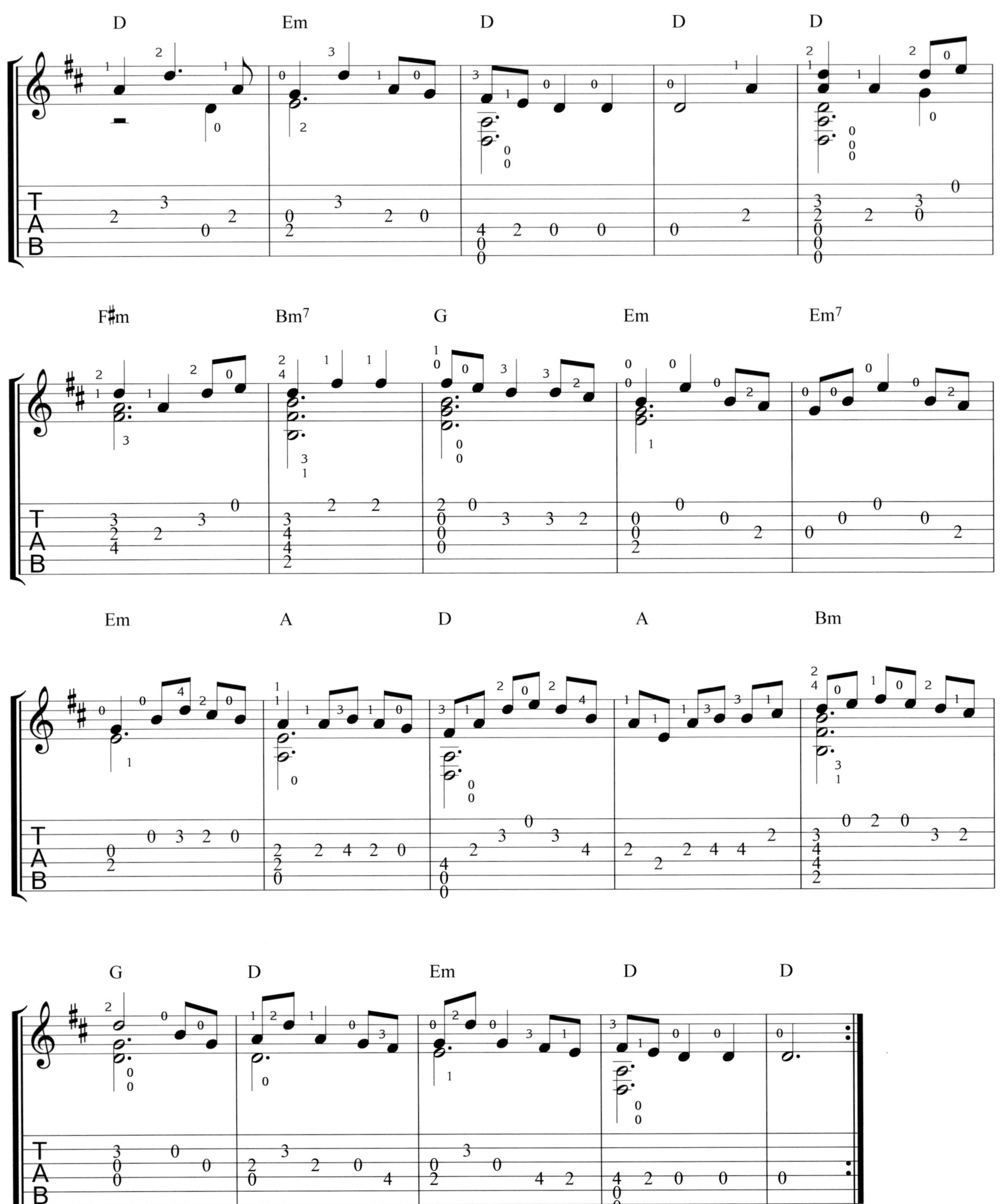
D
Em
D
D
D
F♯m
Bm7
G
Em
Em7
Em
A
D
A
Bm
G
D
Em
D
D
T
A
B

Little Beggarman

Also known as The Red Haired Boy

Traditional Irish

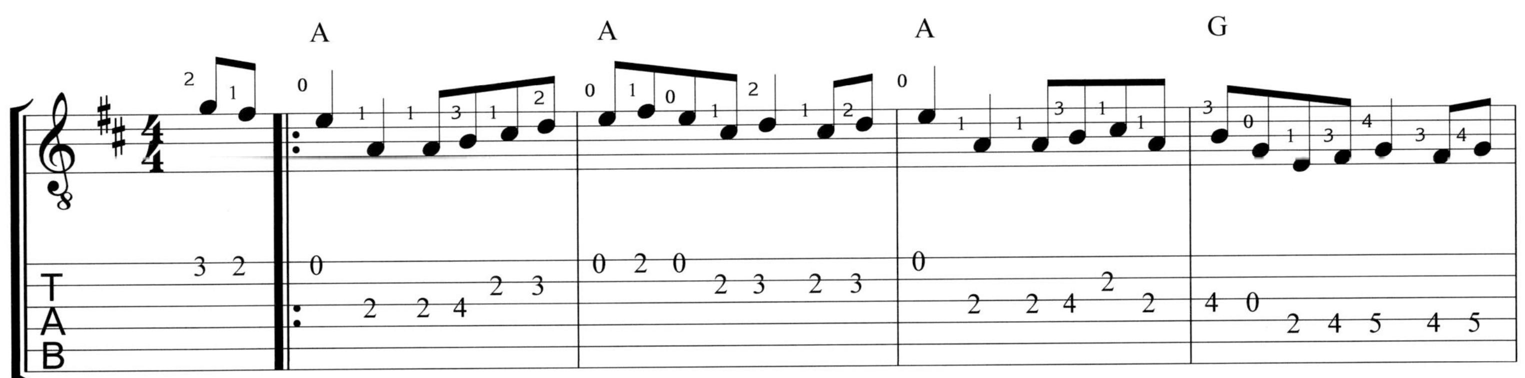

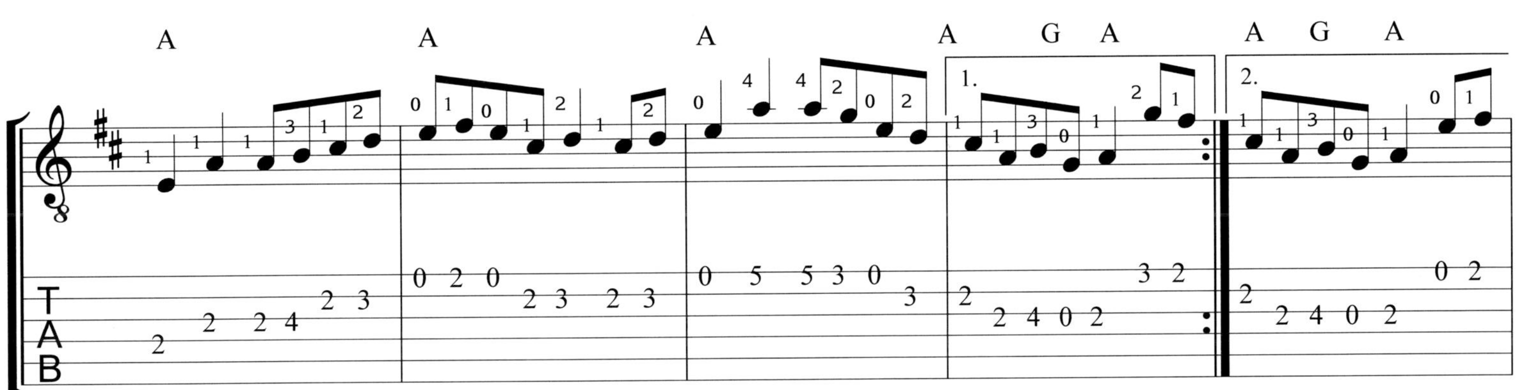

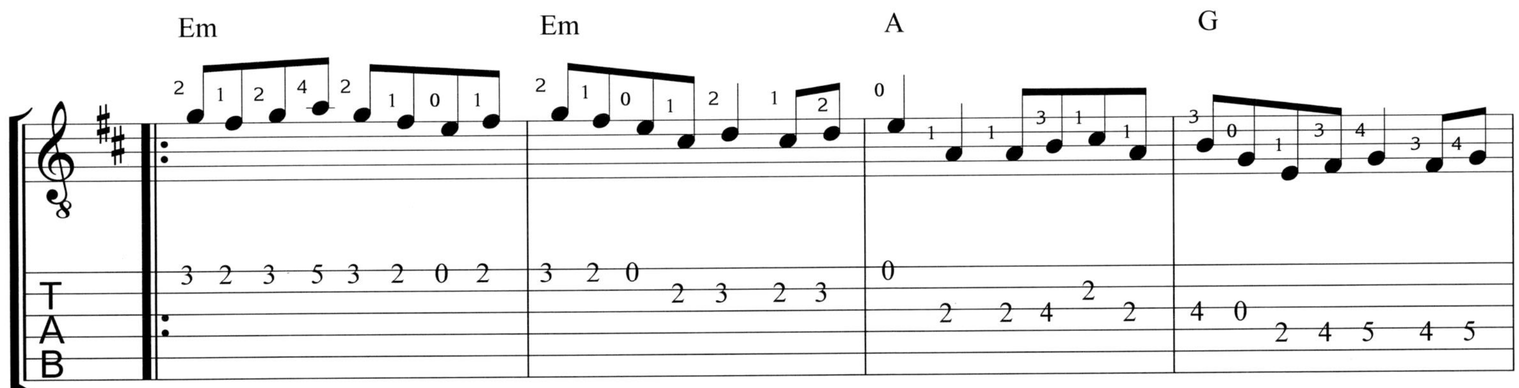

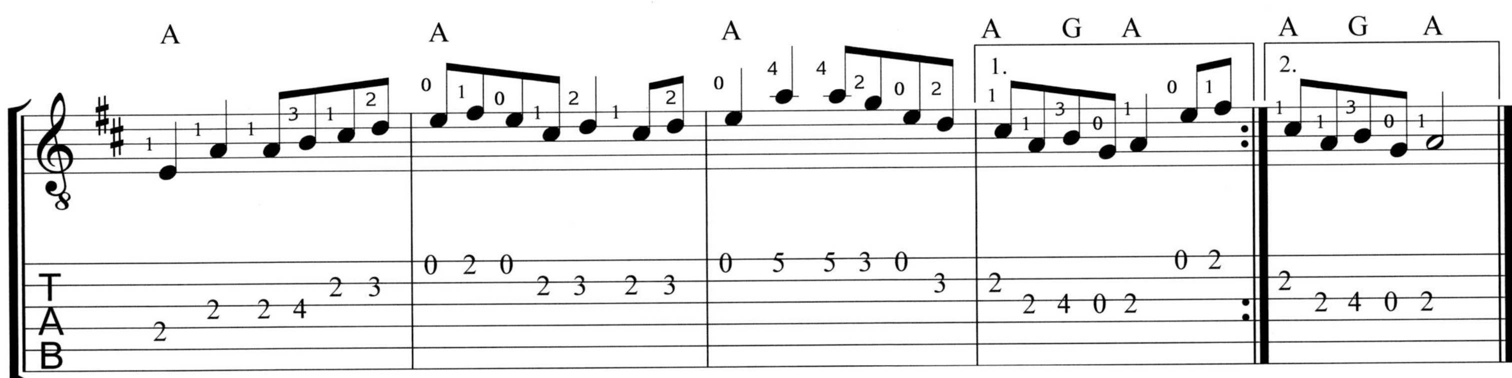

Traditional Irish

Garrett Barry

Arrangement and Variations
by Allan Alexander

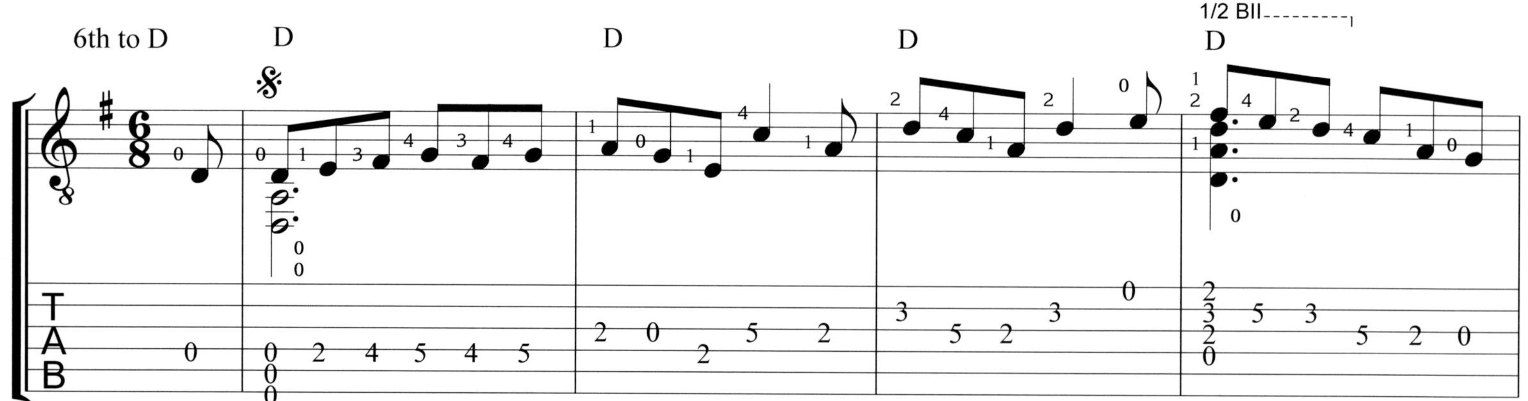

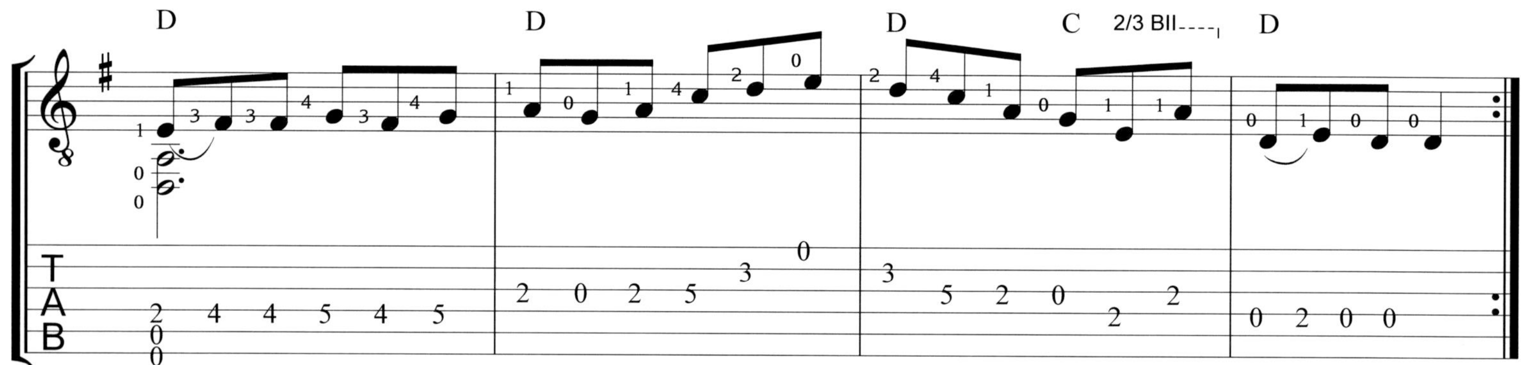

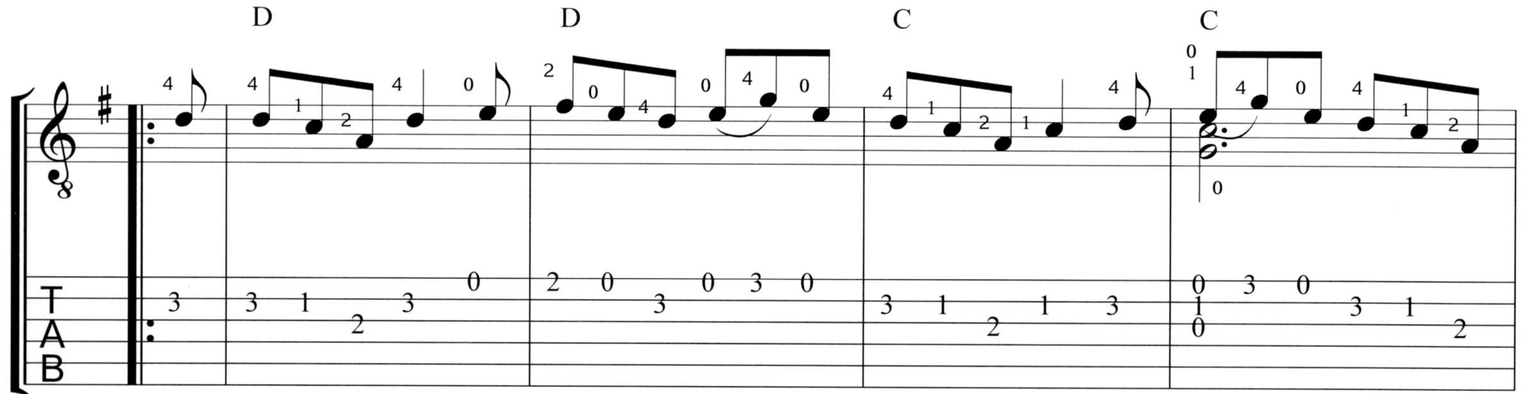

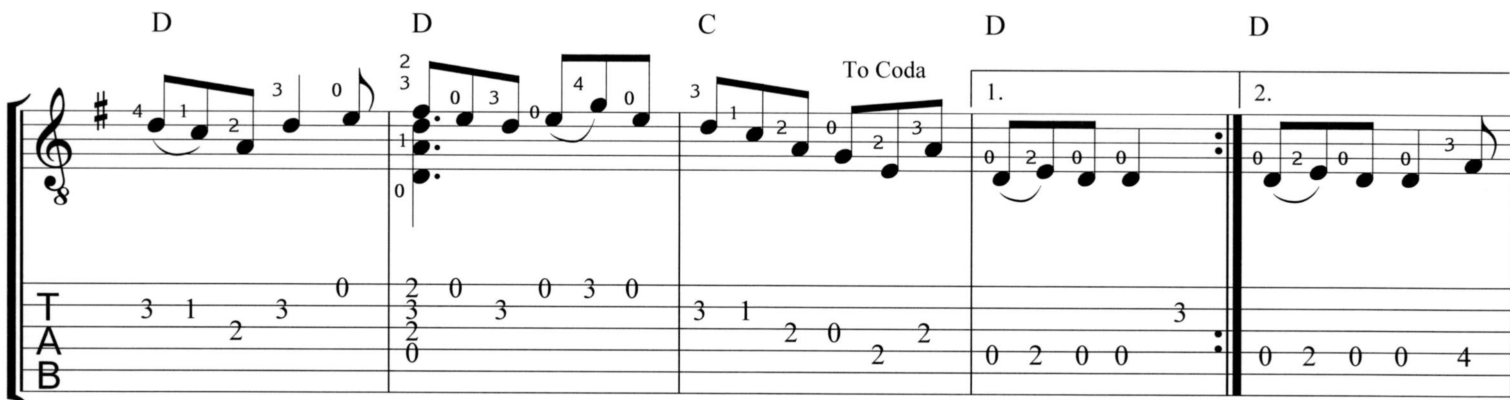

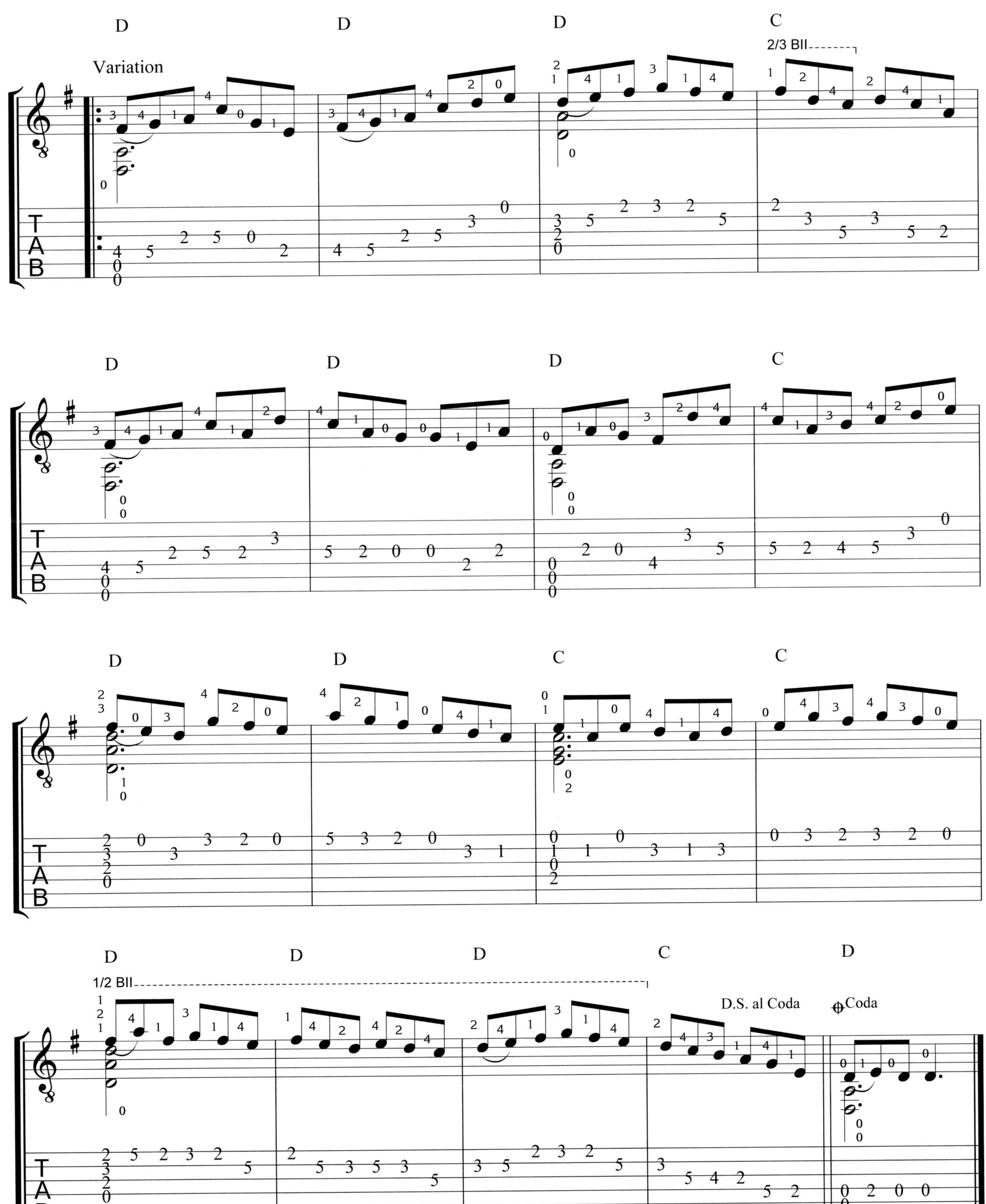

Variation
D
C
2/3 BII
1/2 BII
D.S. al Coda
Coda
T
A
B

Fisherman's Lilt

Arrangement & Variations by
Allan Alexander

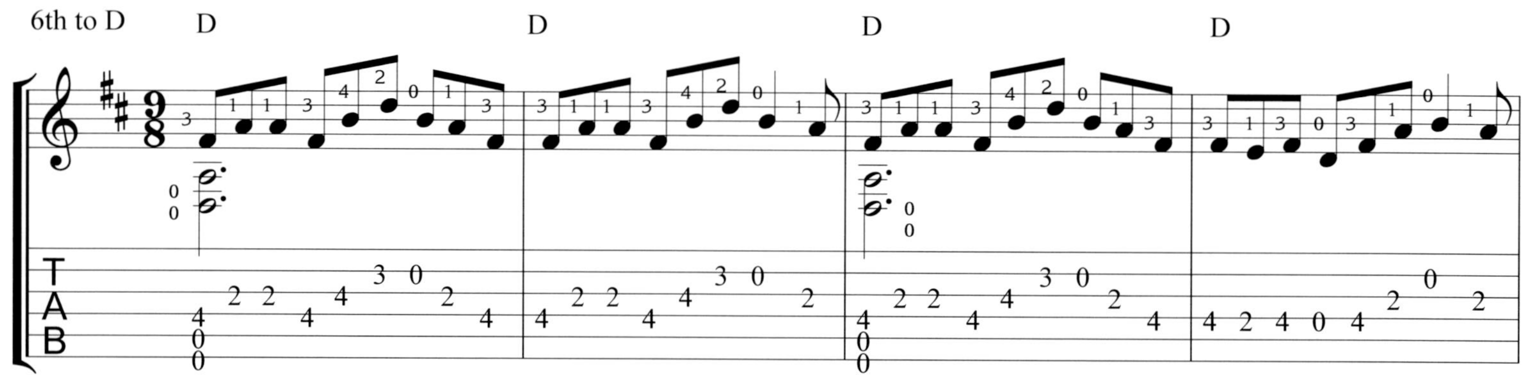

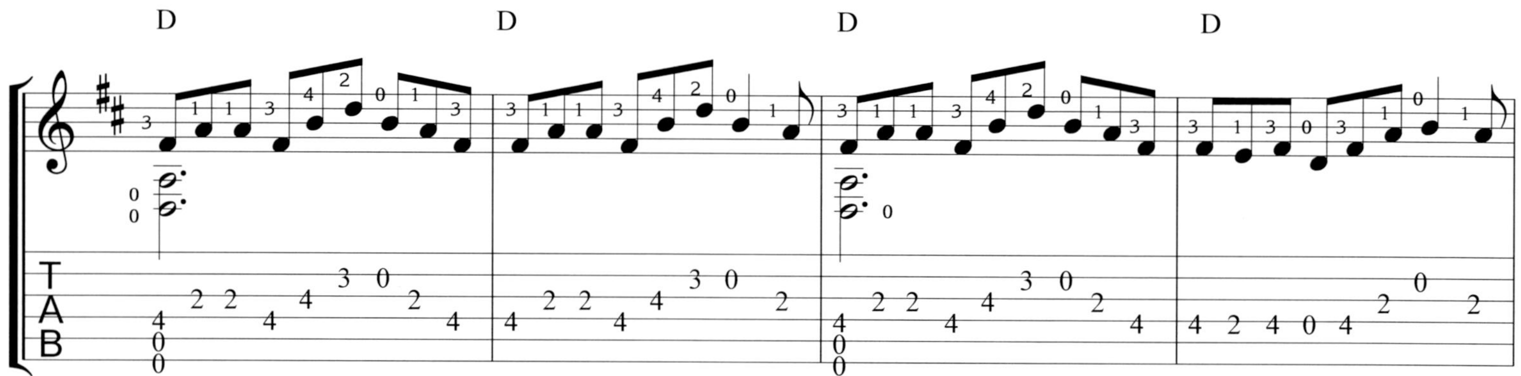

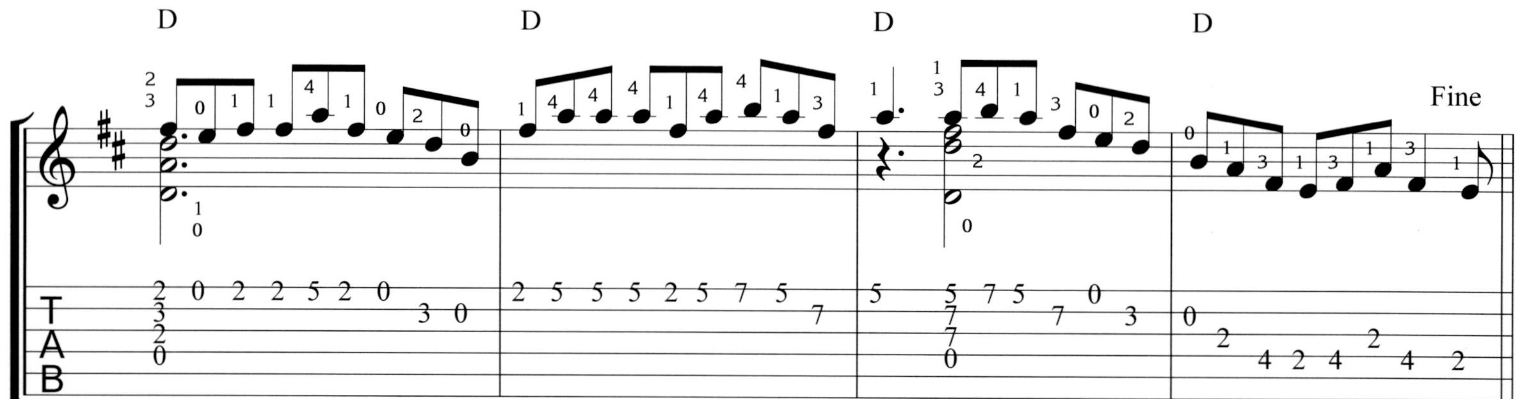

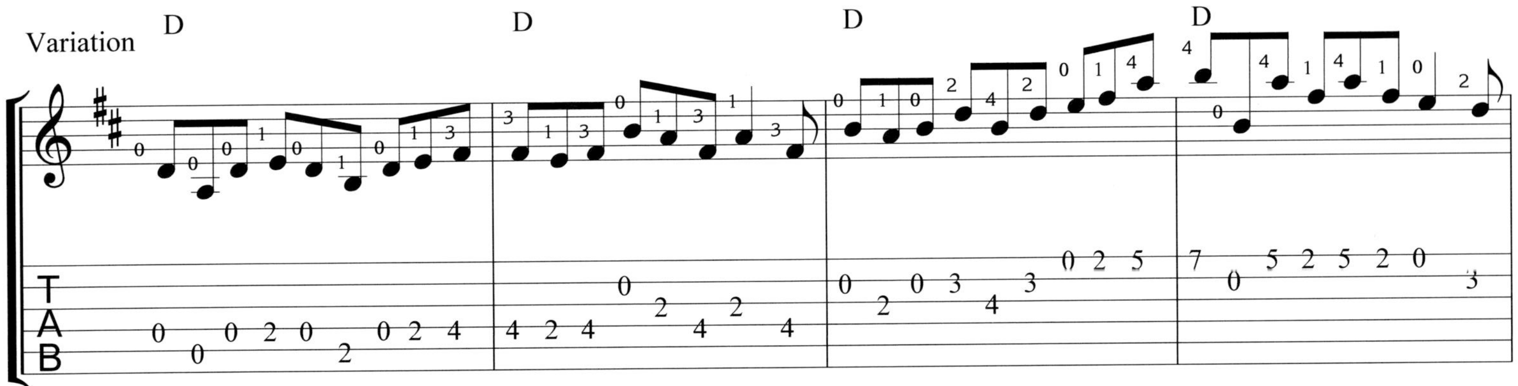
Variation
D
D
D
D
T
A
B

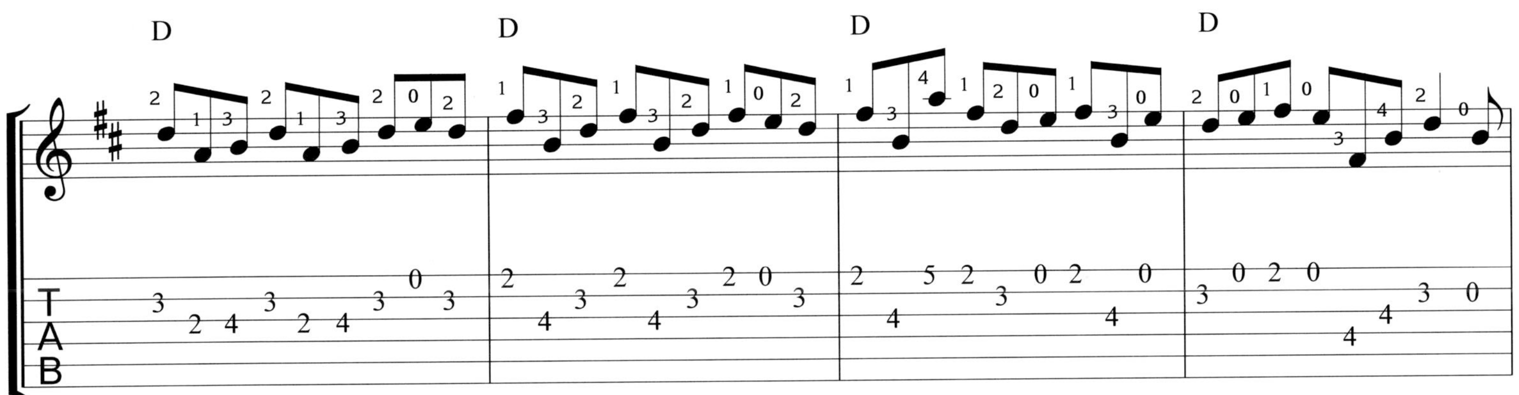
D
D
D
D
T
A
B

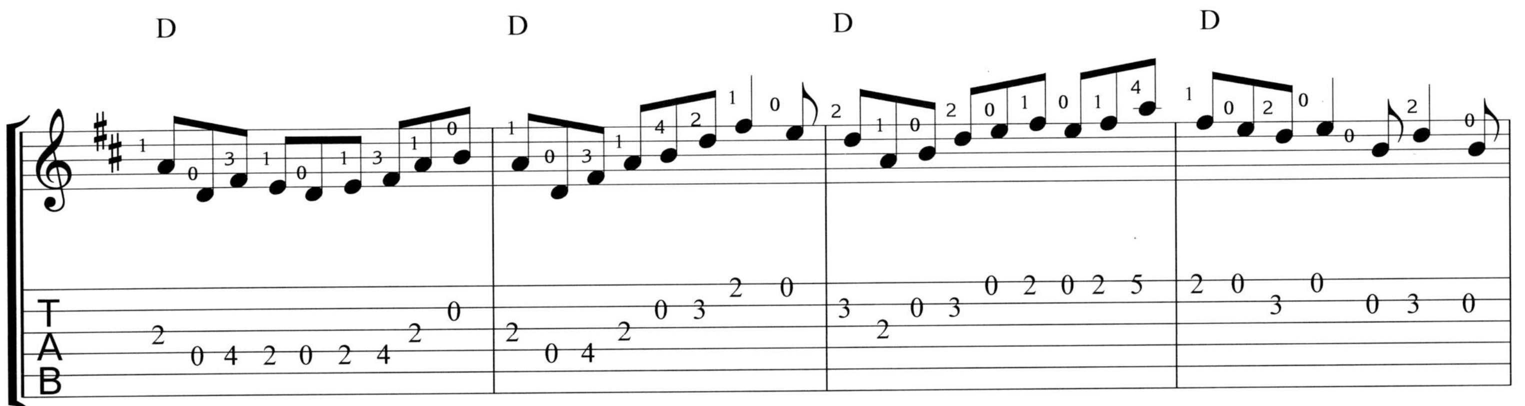
D
D
D
D
T
A
B

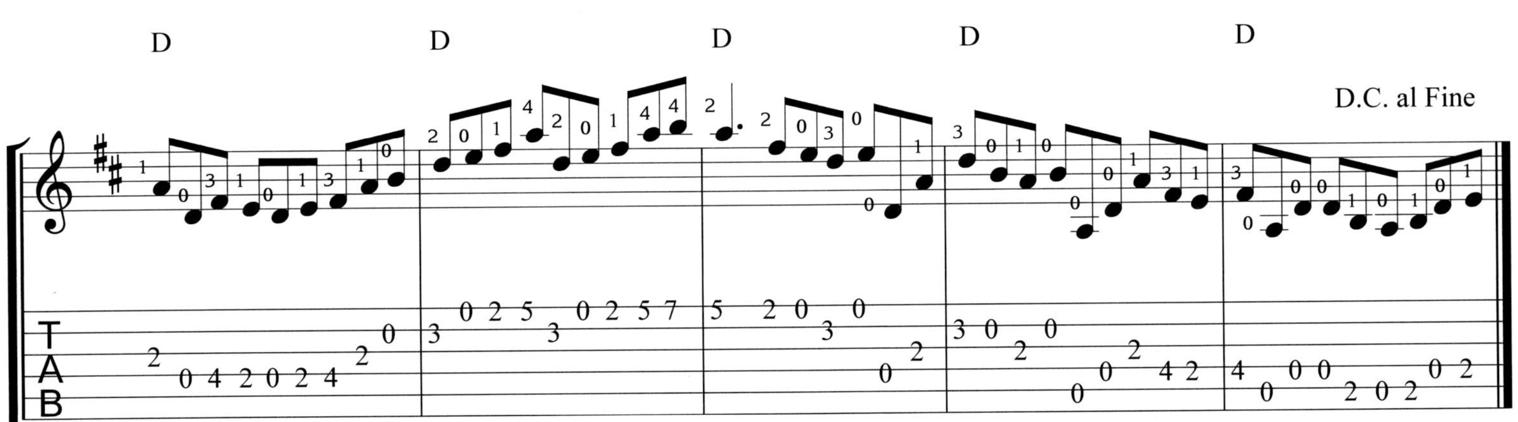
D
D
D
D
D
D.C. al Fine
T
A
B

Turlough Carolan

Eleanor Plunkett

Arrangement & Variation by
Allan Alexander

6th to D

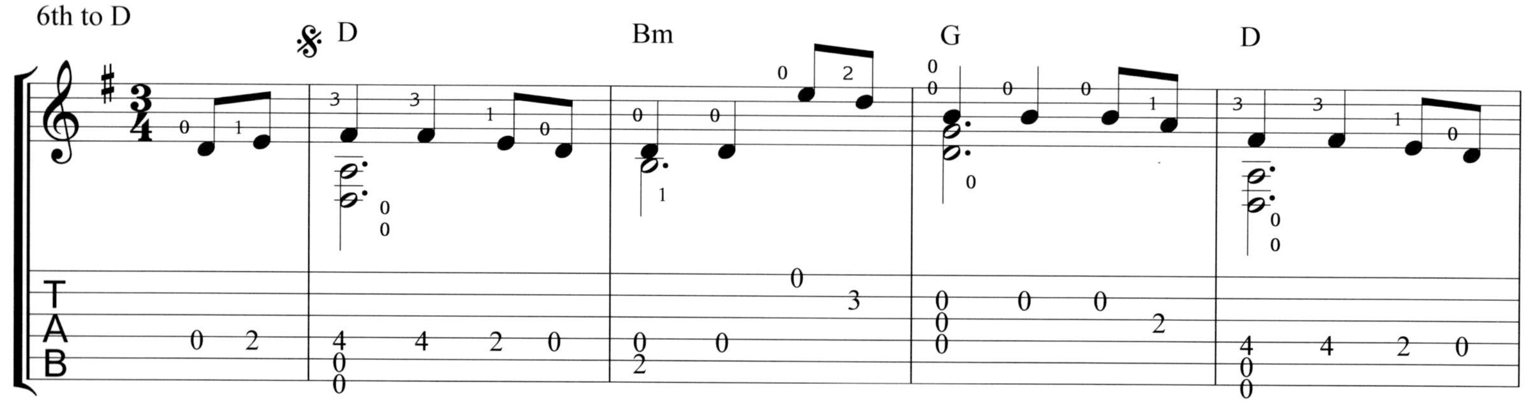

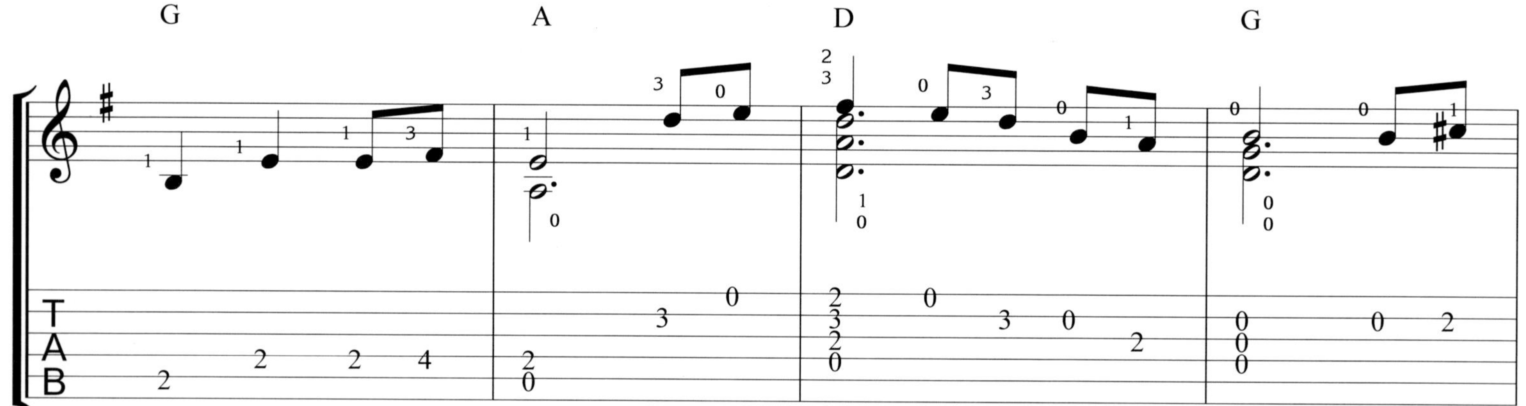

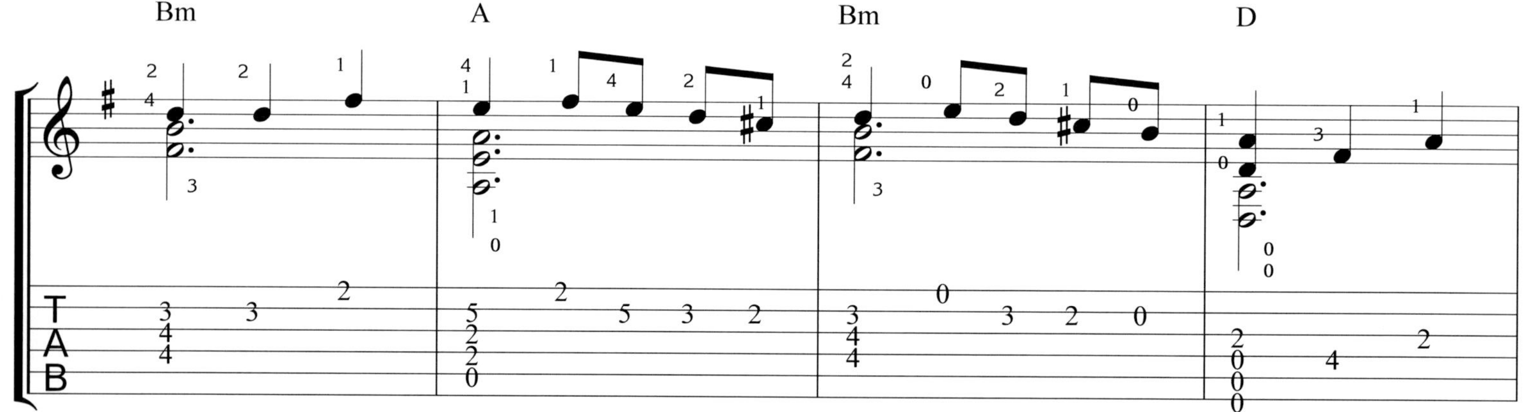

Variation
BII
D
Bm
G
D
G
A
D
G
Bm
A
Bm
D
G
D
G
A
D.S. al Fine

Dermott O'Doud

Turlough Carolan

Arrangement and Variations by
Allan Alexander

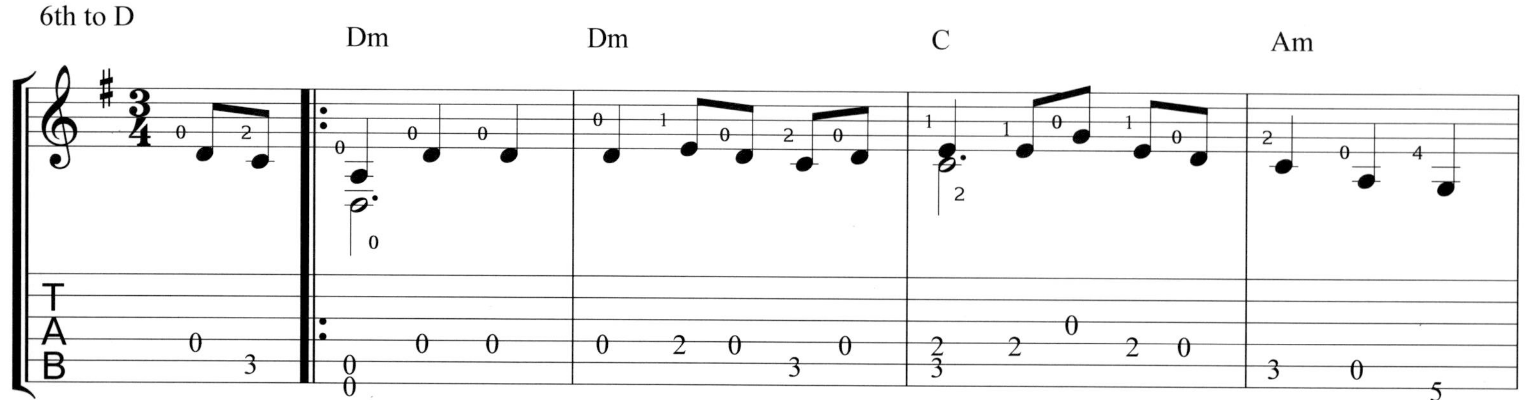

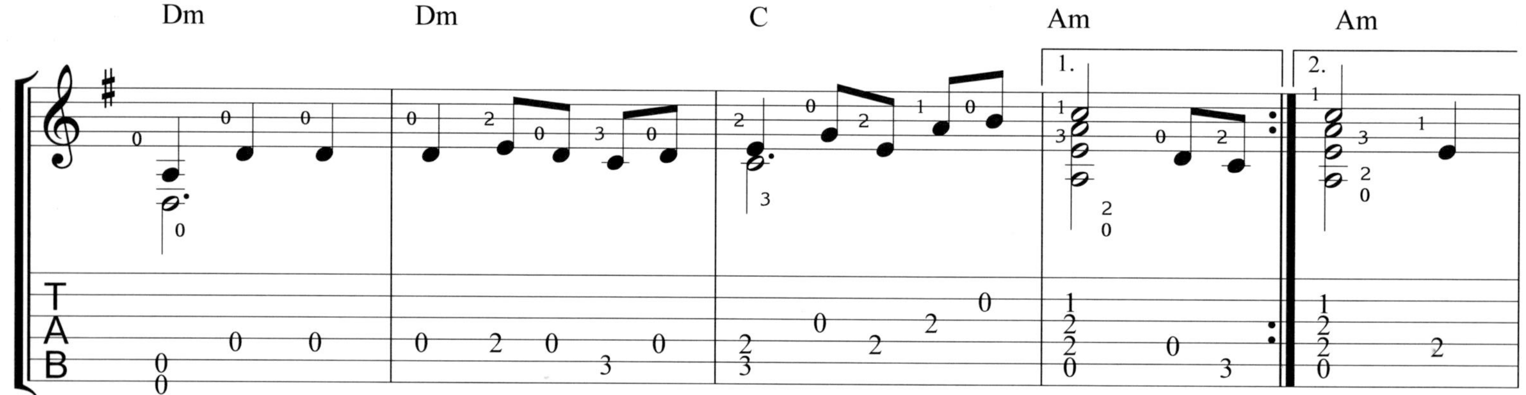

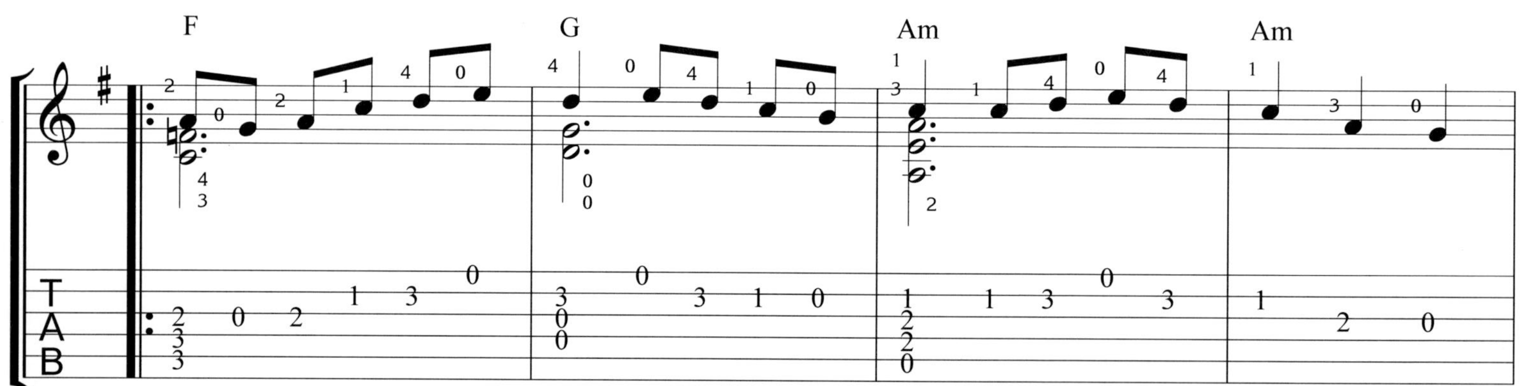

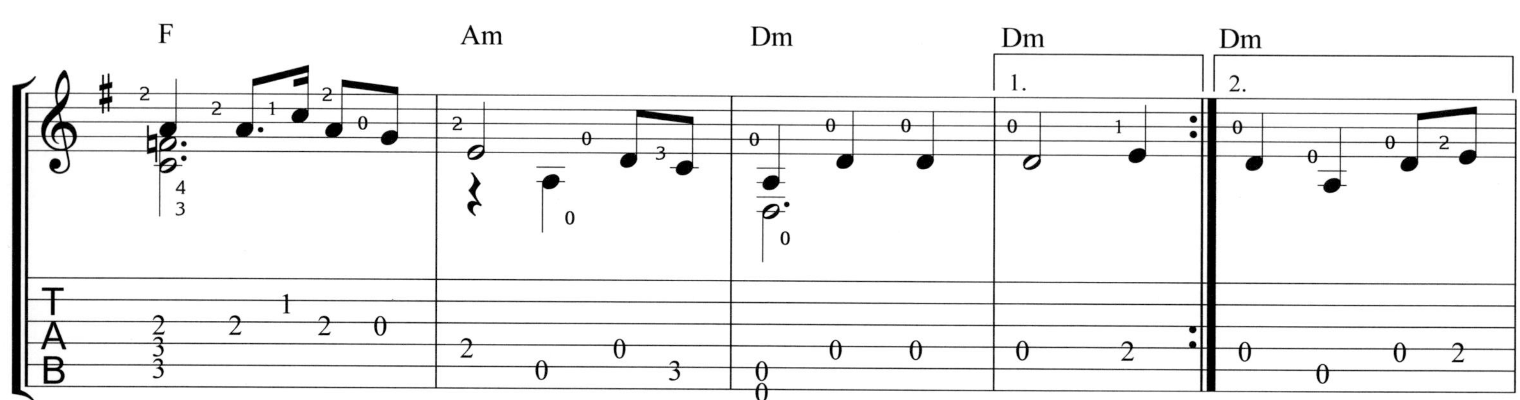

Variation

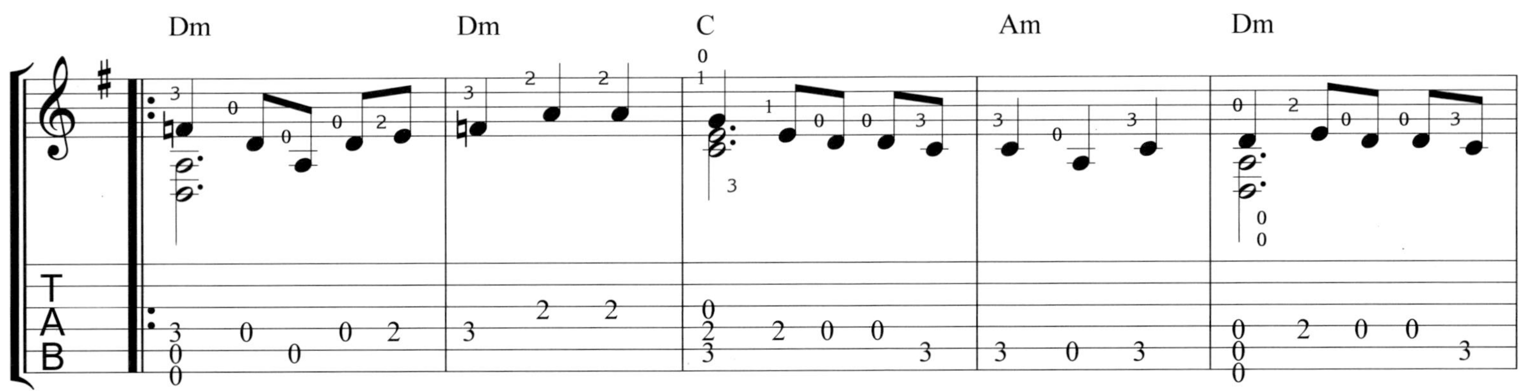

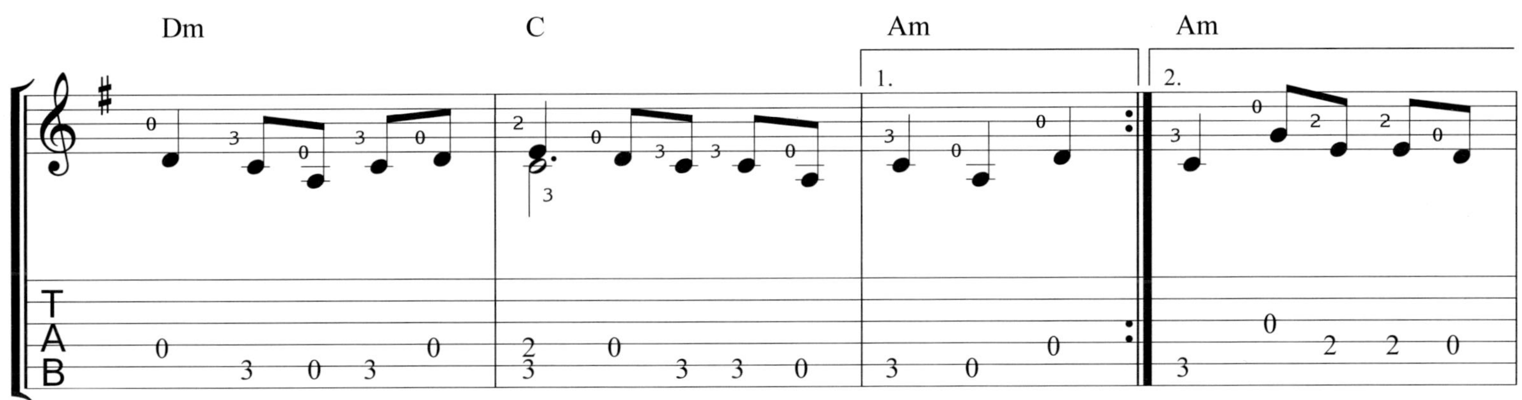

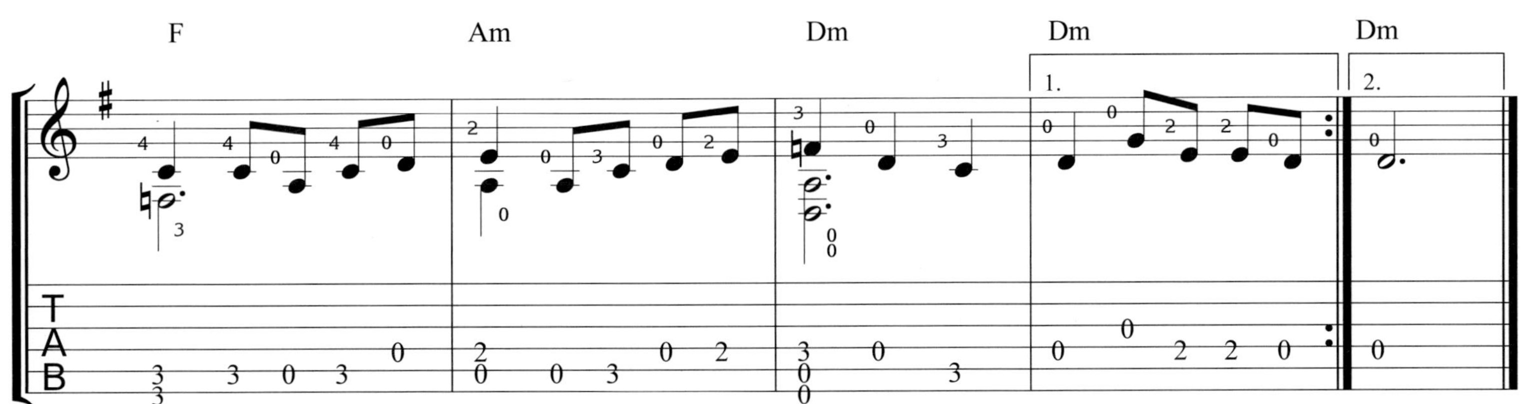

Cremonea

Turlough Carolan

Arrangement & Variations by
Allan Alexander

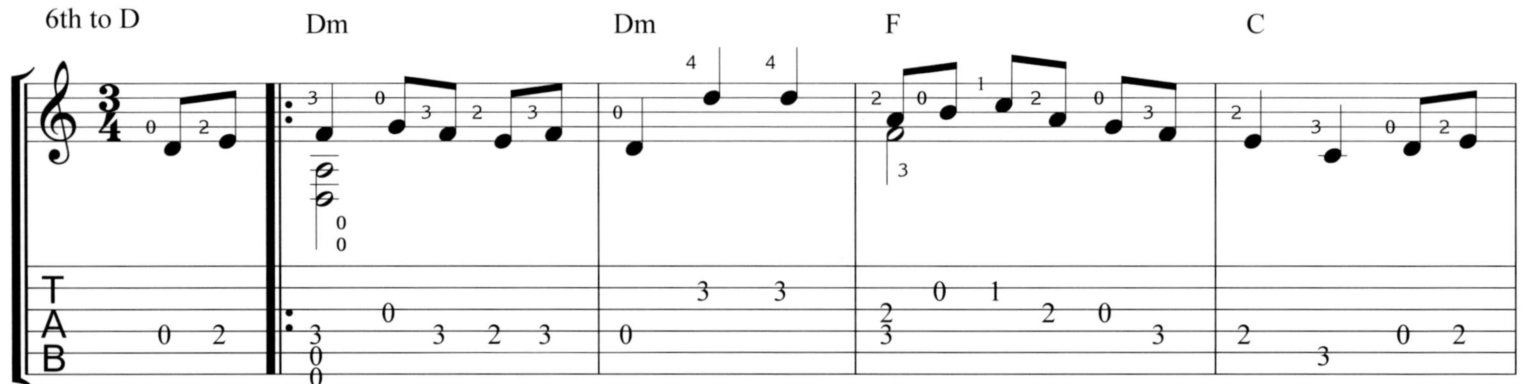

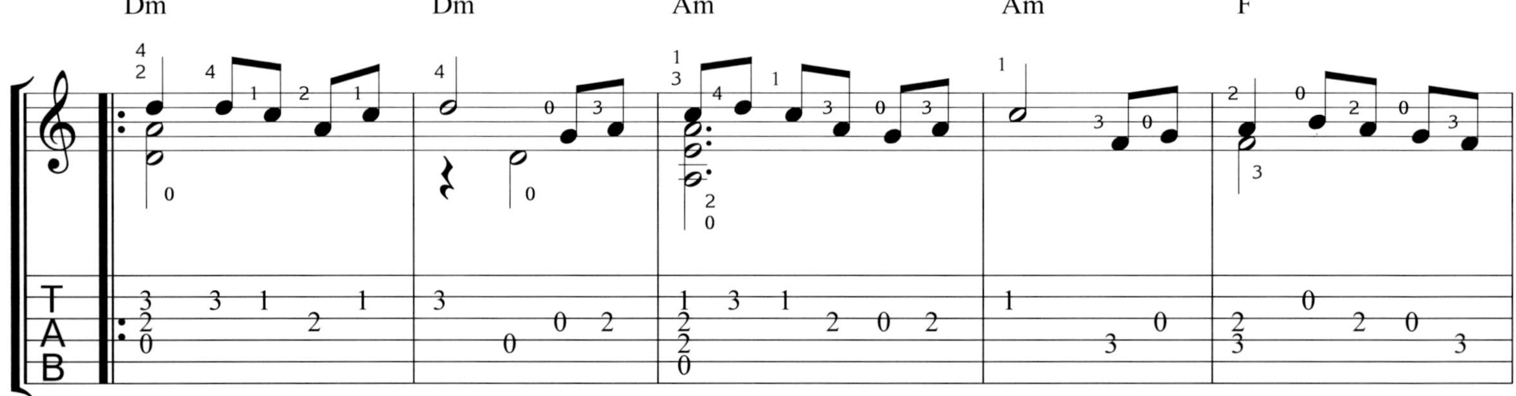

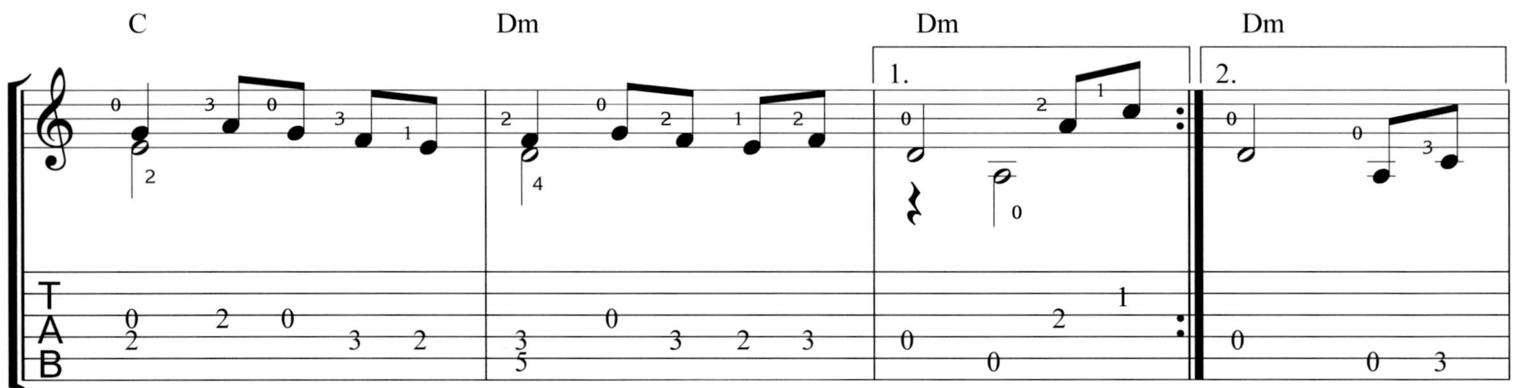

Variation

Song of the Chanter

Arrangement & Variations by
Allan Alexander & Jessica Walsh

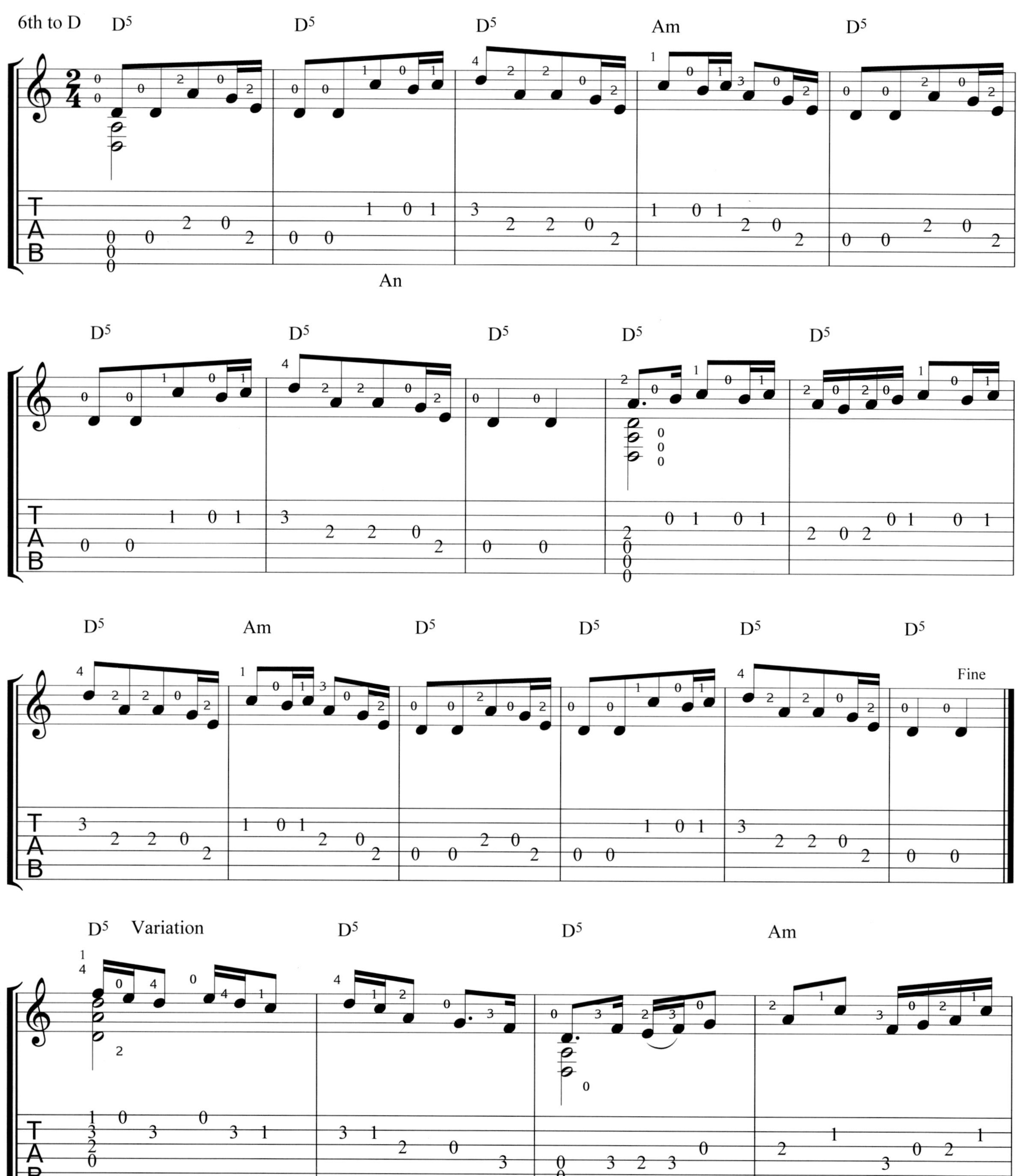

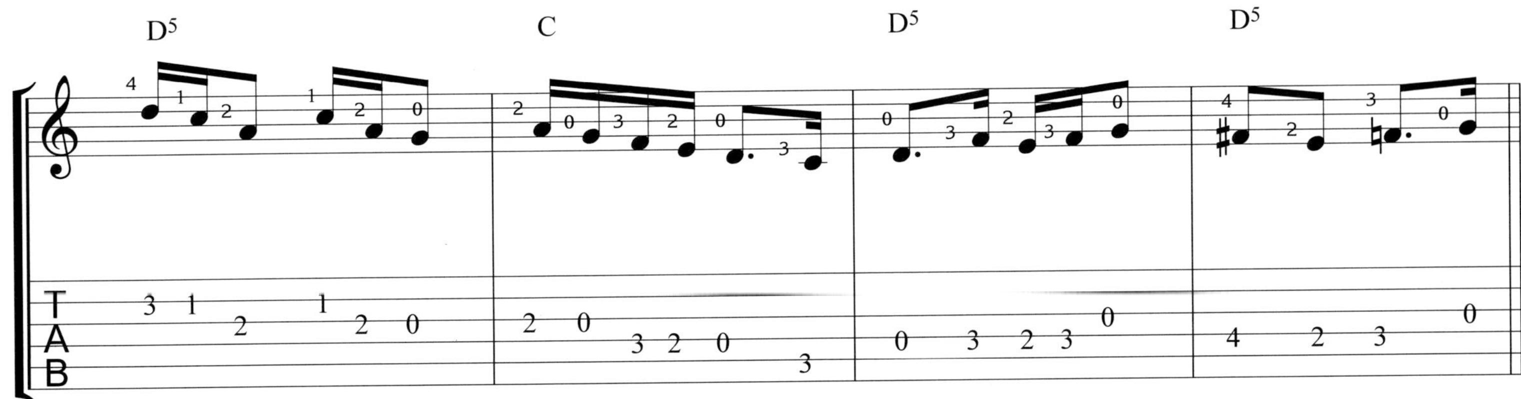
D5
C
D5
D5

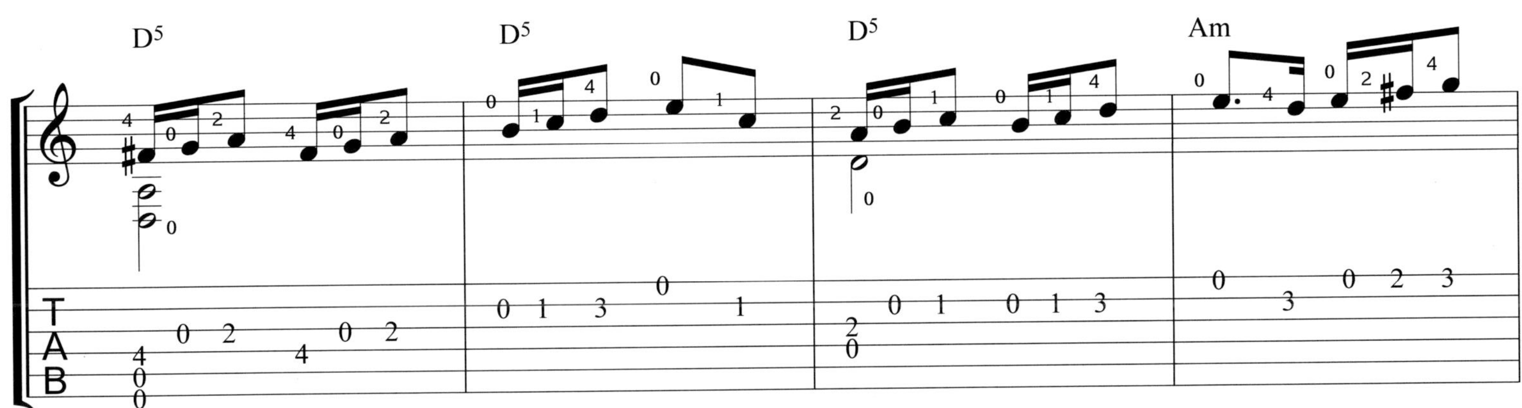
D5
D5
D5
Am

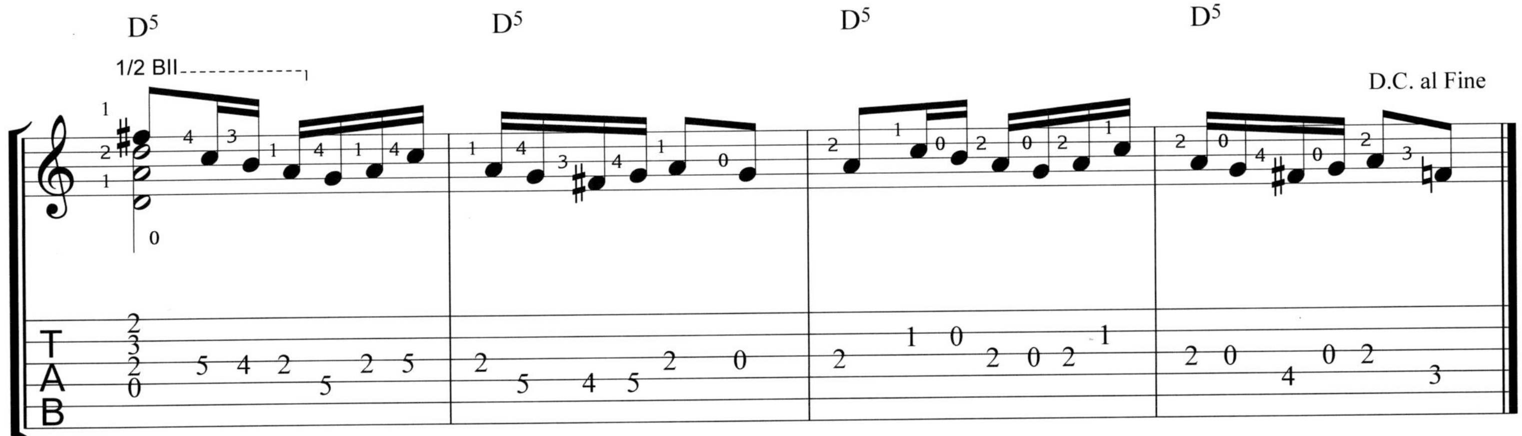
D5
D5
D5
D5
1/2 BII
D.C. al Fine

A Toy

From Jane Pickering's Lute Book -
Setting & Variations by Allan Alexander

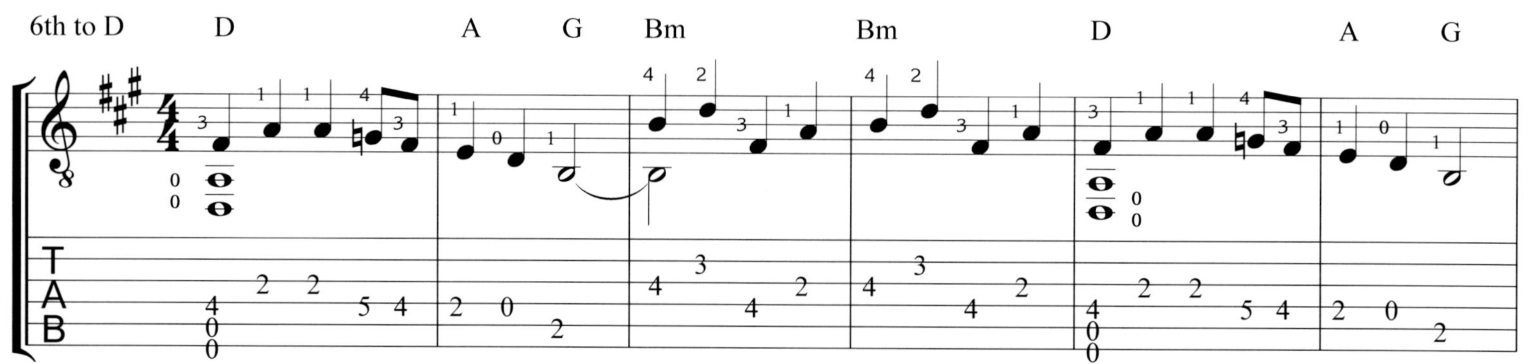

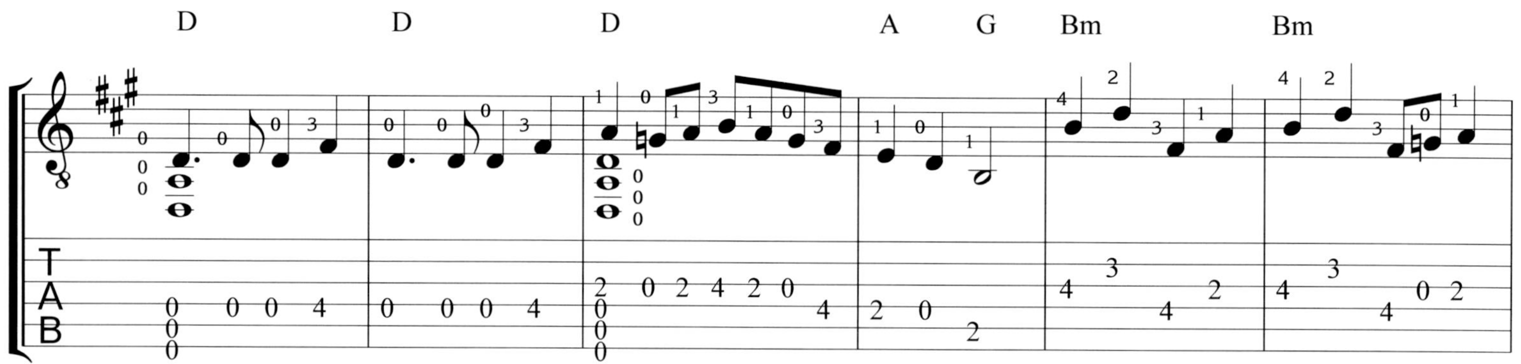

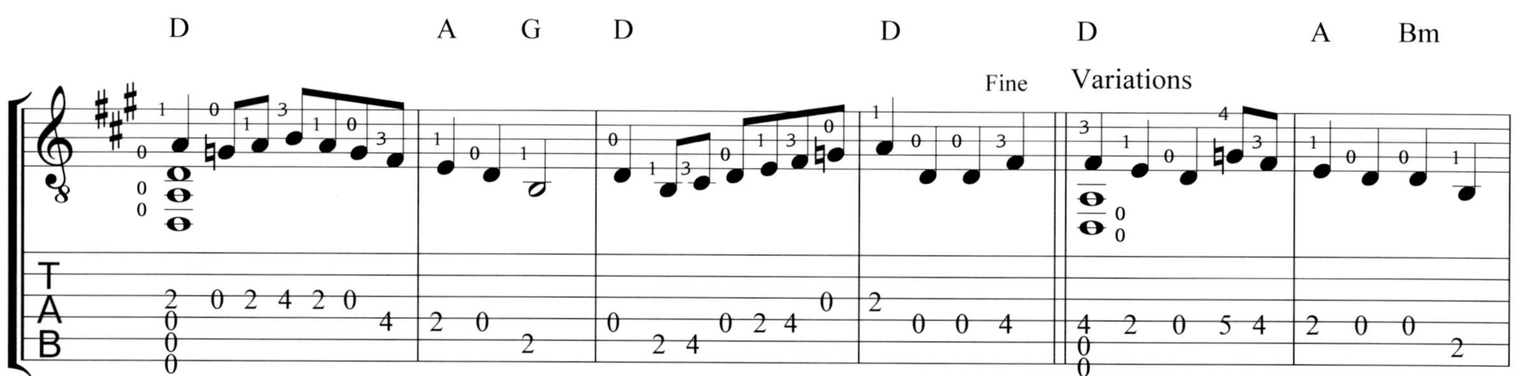

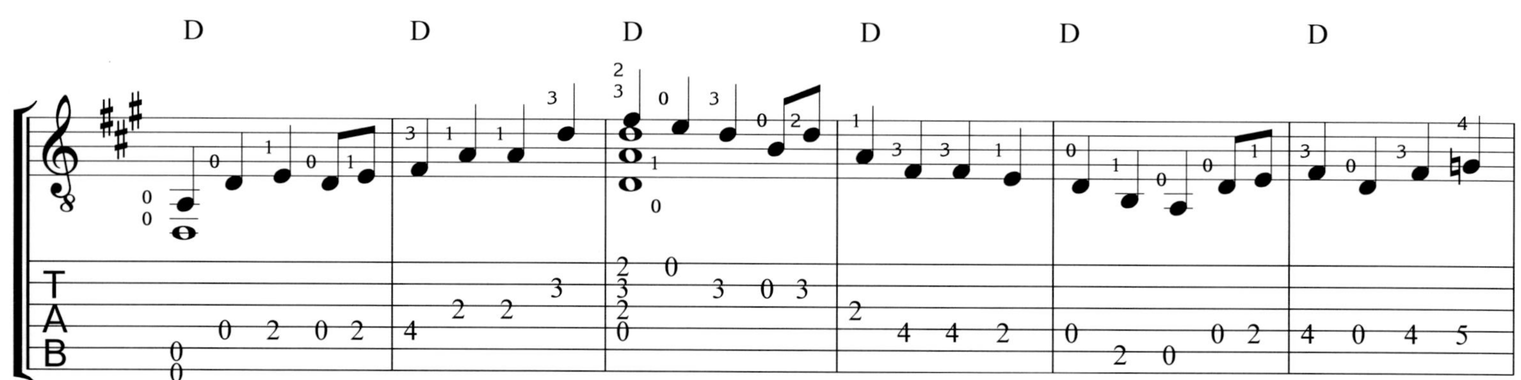

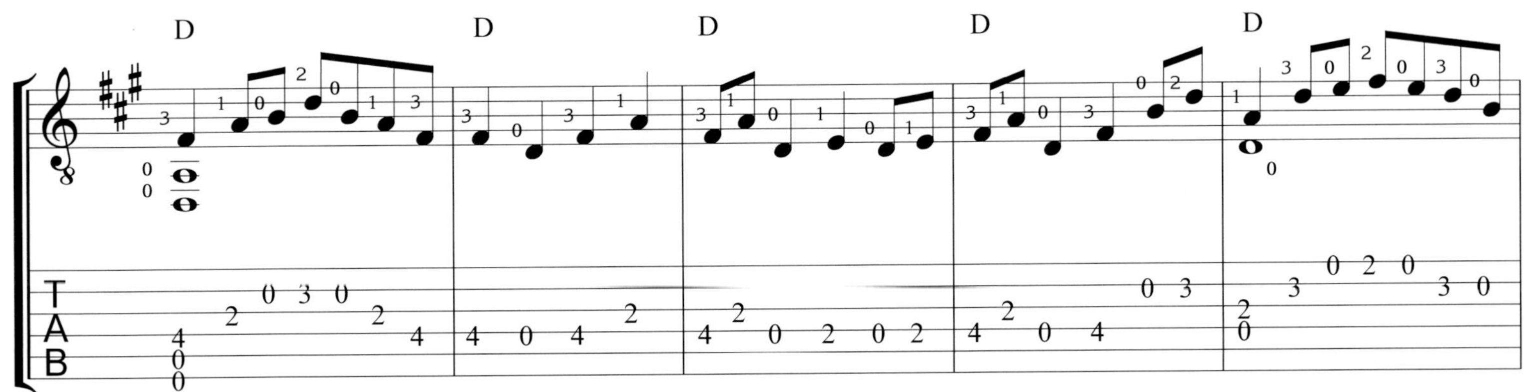
D
D
D
D
D
T
A
B

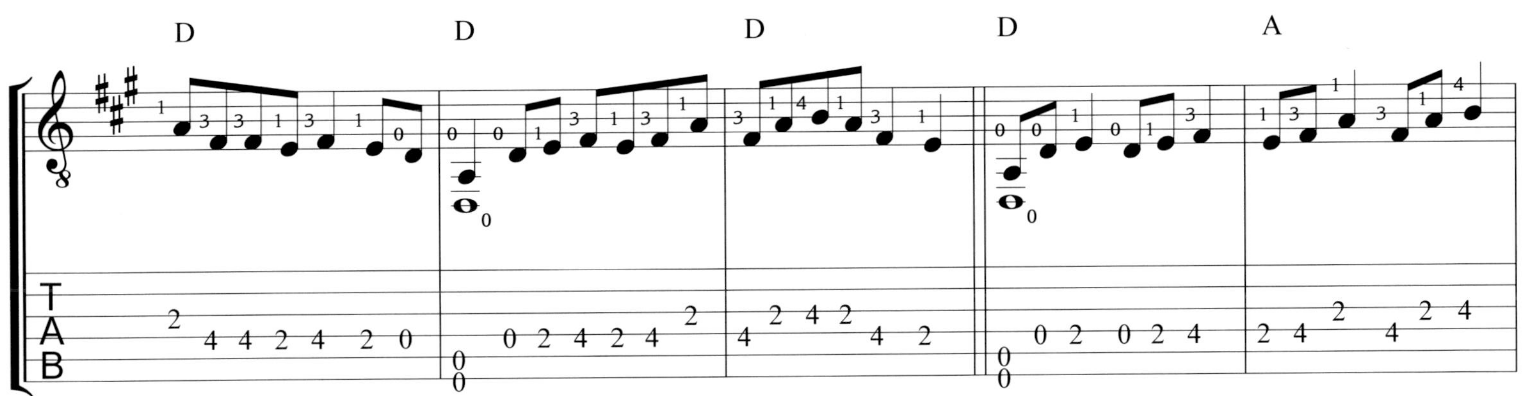
D
D
D
D
A
T
A
B

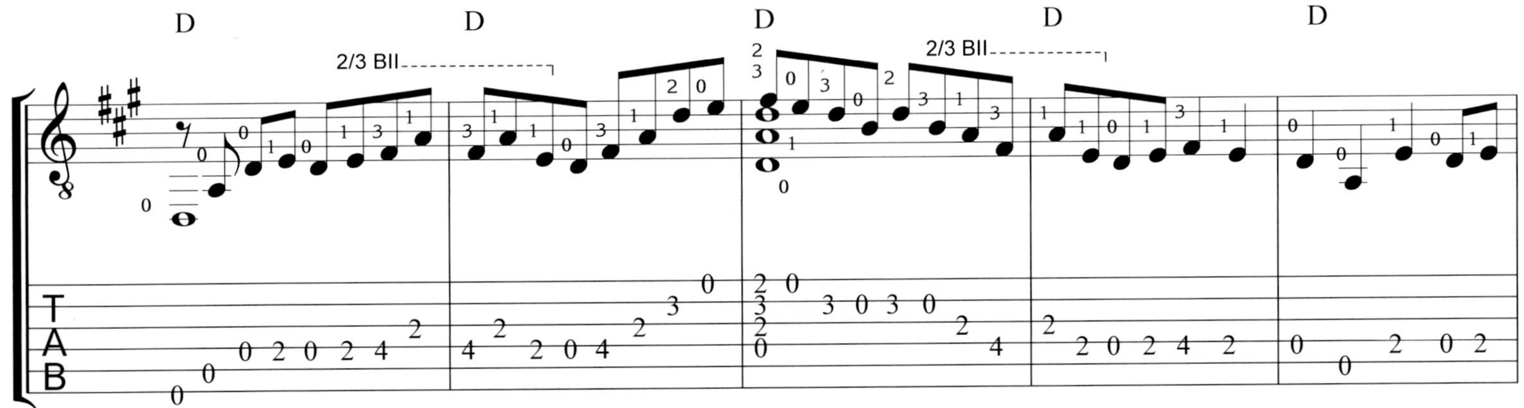
D
2/3 BII
D
D
2/3 BII
D
D
T
A
B

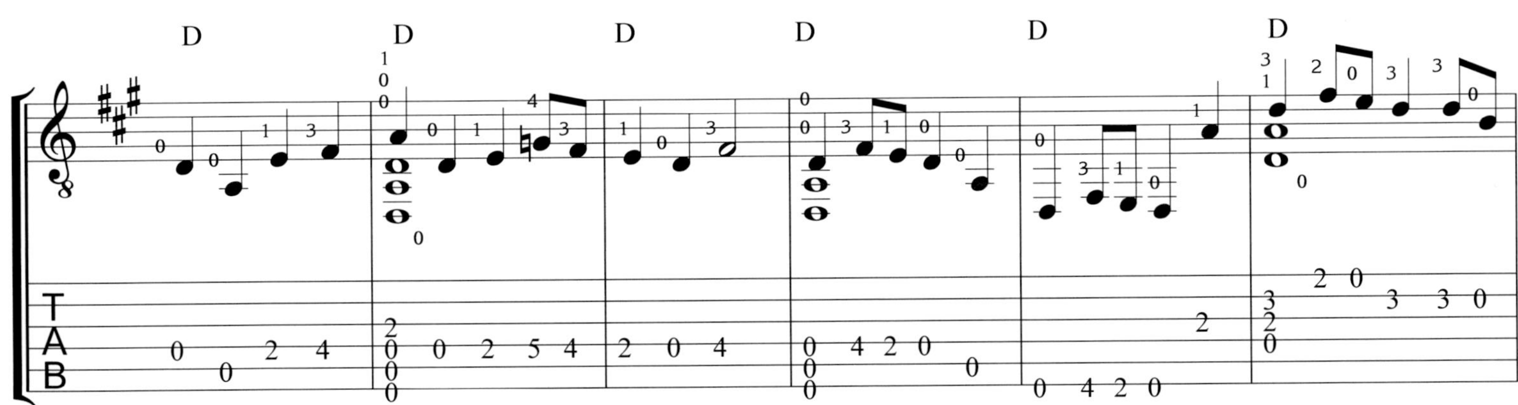
D
D
D
D
D
D
T
A
B

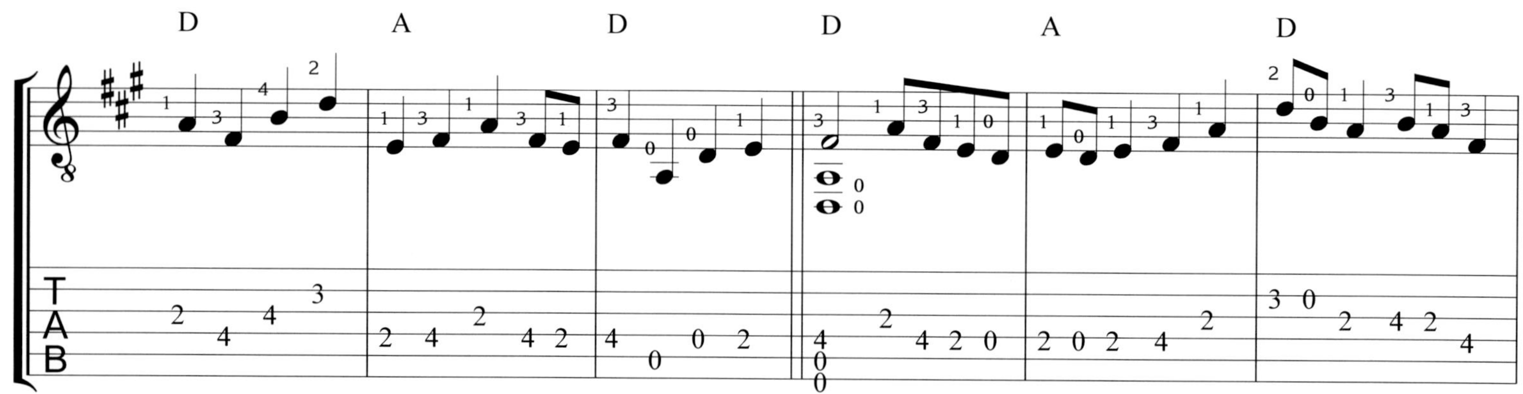
D
A
D
D
A
D

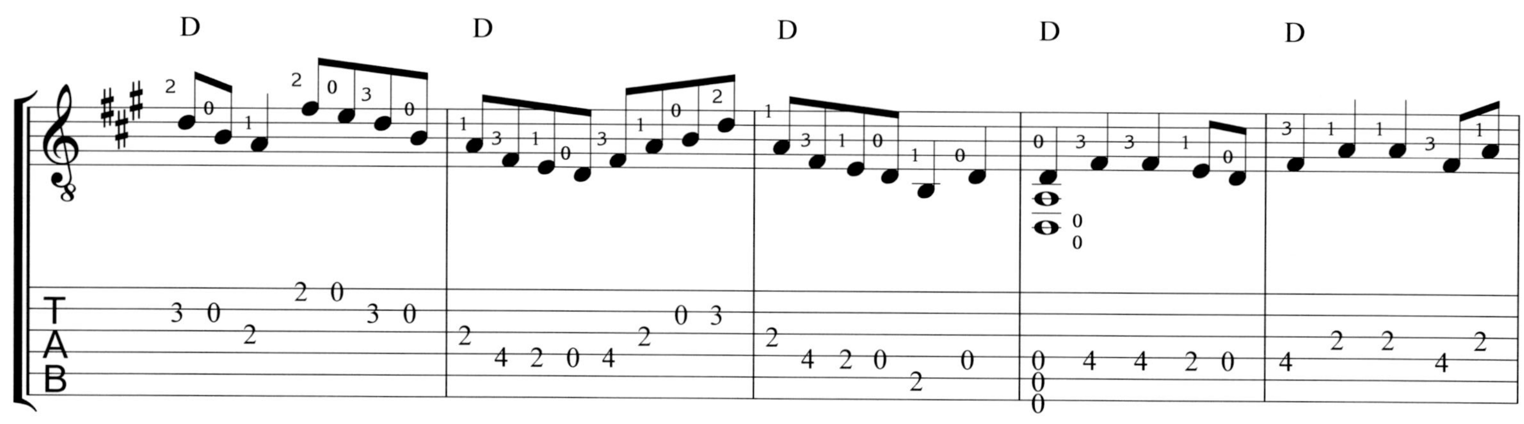
D
D
D
D
D

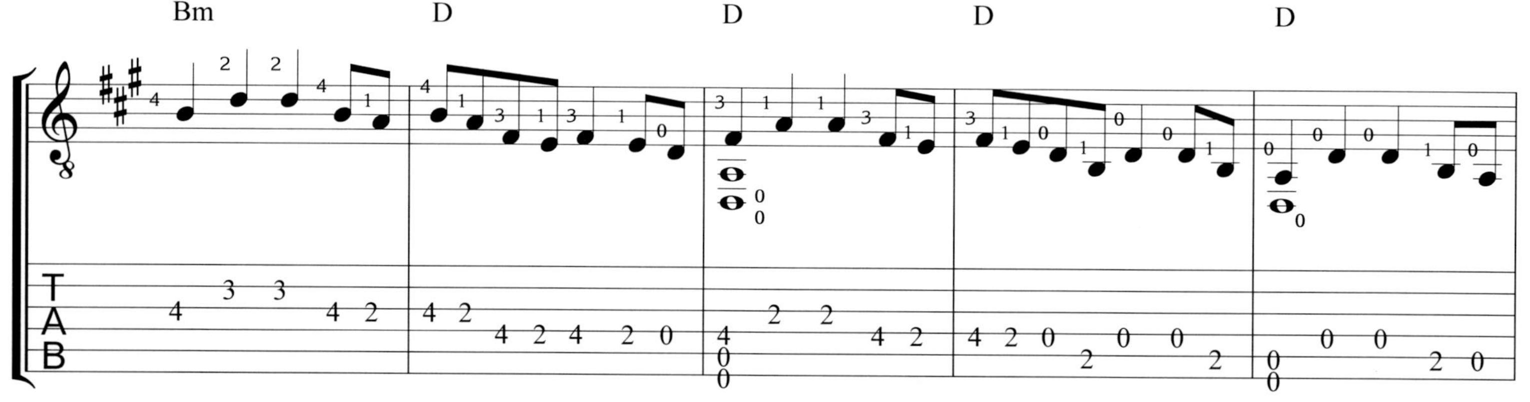
Bm
D
D
D
D

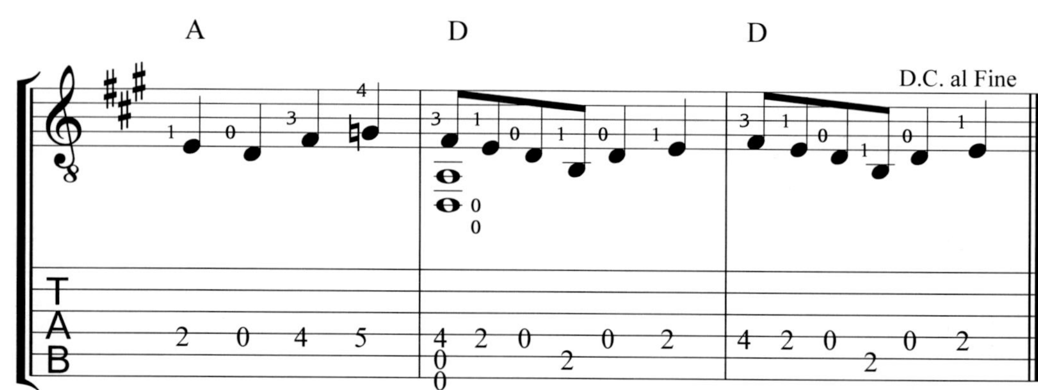
A
D
D
D.C. al Fine

Separation of Soul and Body

Turlough Carolan

Arrangement & Variation
by Allan Alexander

Lilt Milne

From the Wemyss Lute Book

Setting & Variation by
Allan Alexander

6th to D

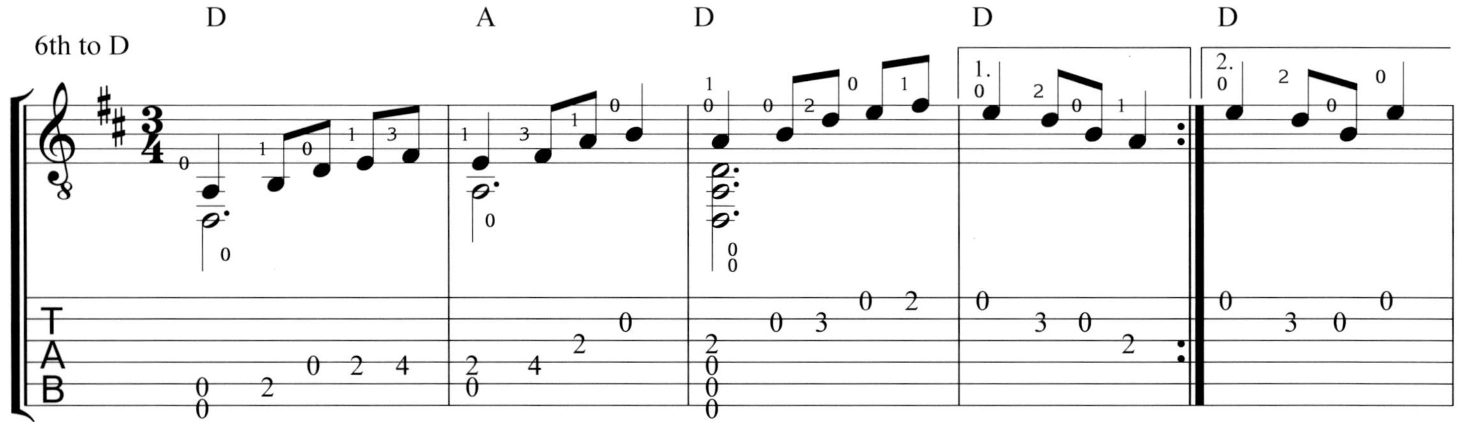

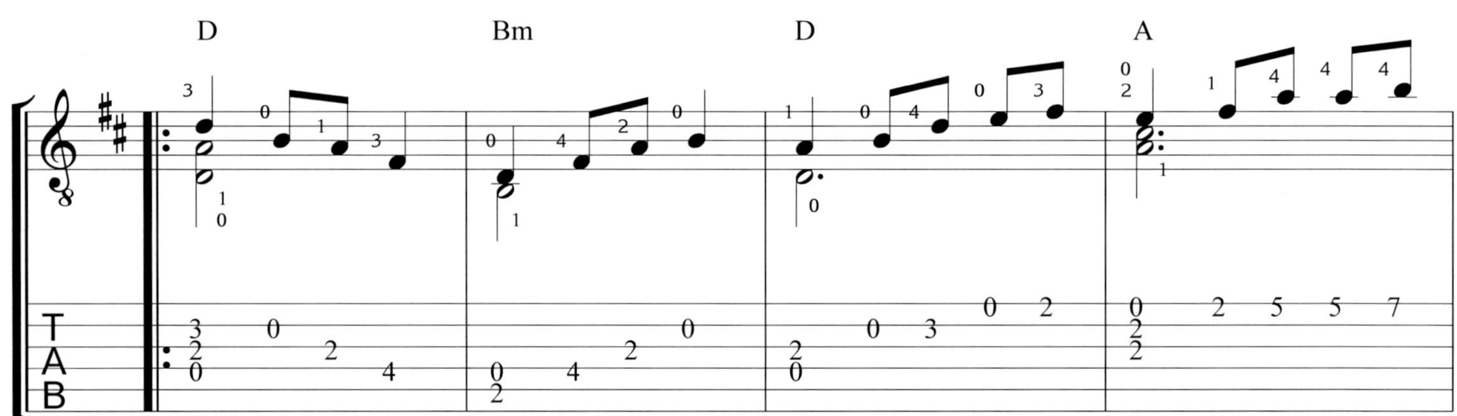

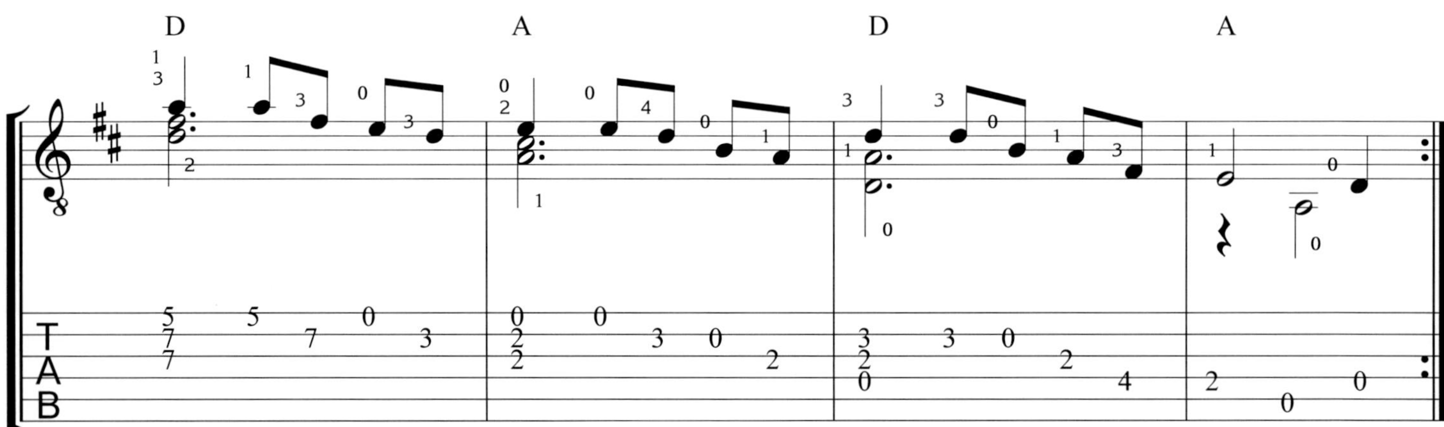

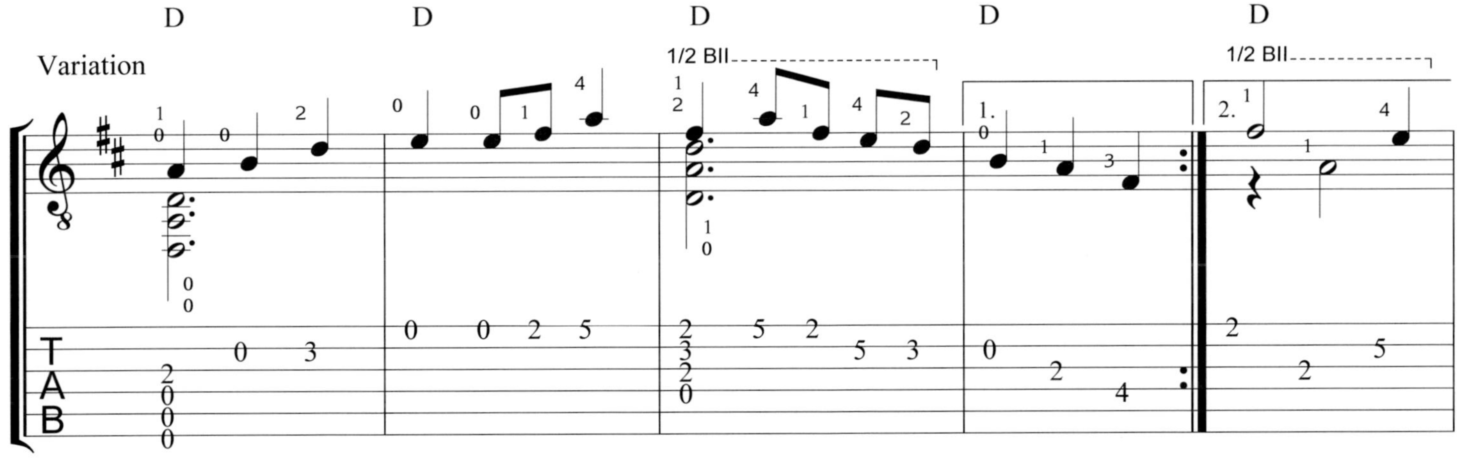
Variation
D
D
D
D
D
1/2 BII
1/2 BII
1.
2.
T
A
B

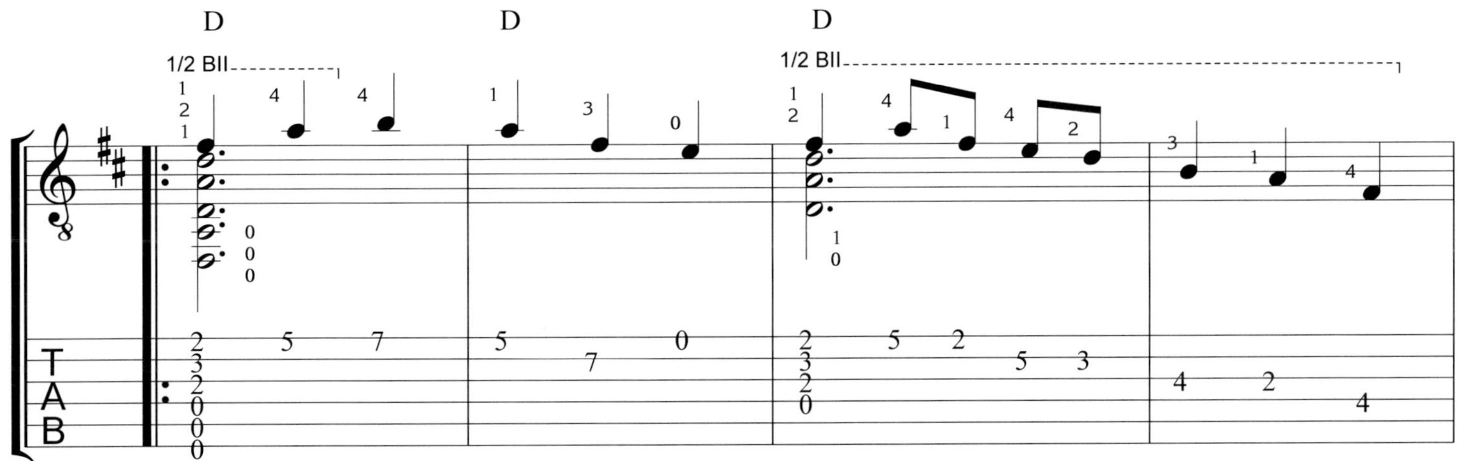
D
D
D
1/2 BII
1/2 BII
T
A
B

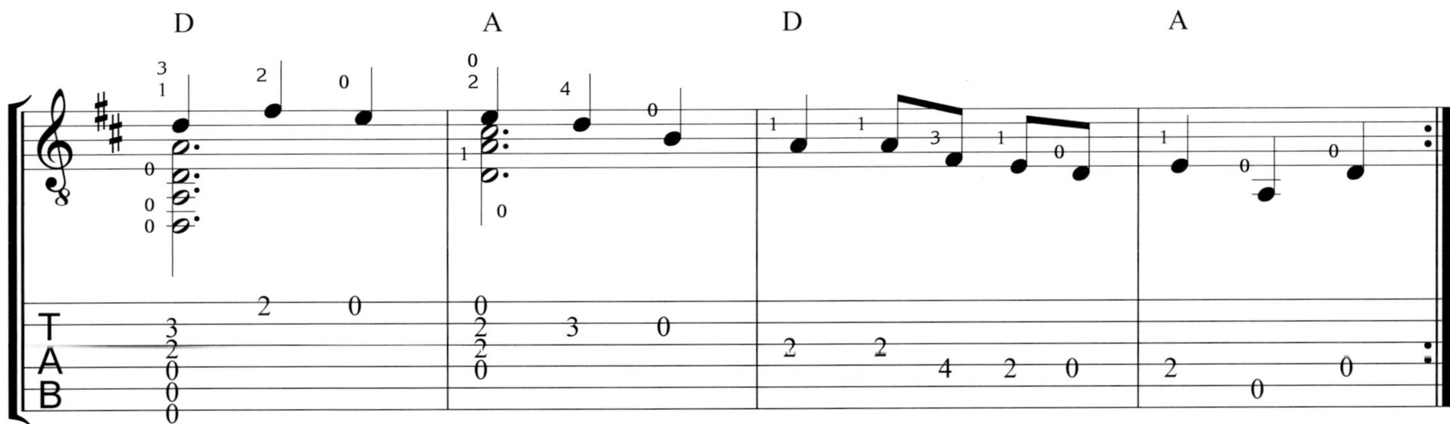
D
A
D
A
T
A
B

Wo Betyd Thy Waerie Bodie

From the Straloch Lute Manuscript

Arrangement and Variitions by Allan Alexander

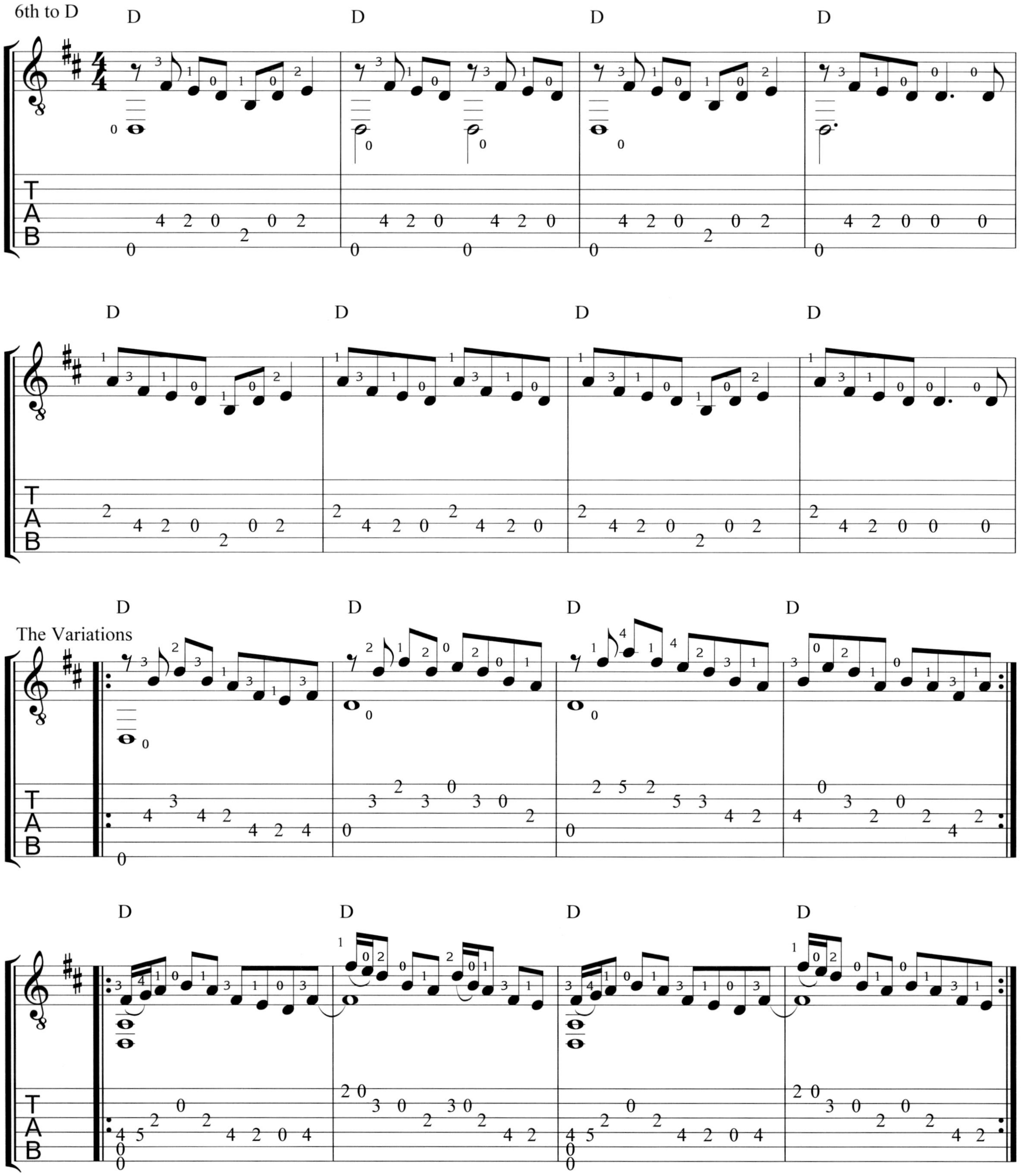
6th to D
D
The Variations
TAB

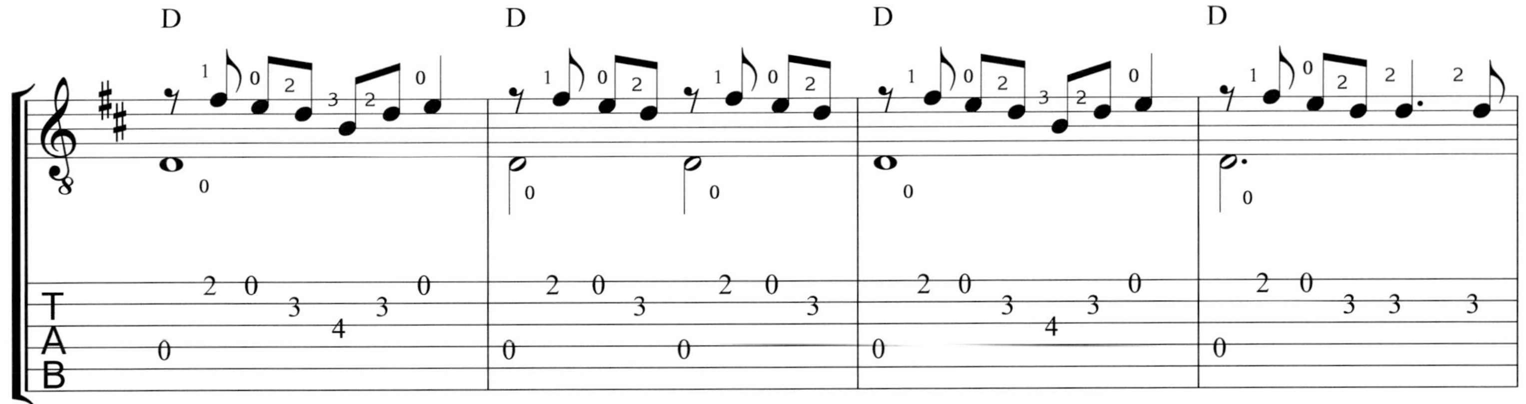
D
D
D
D

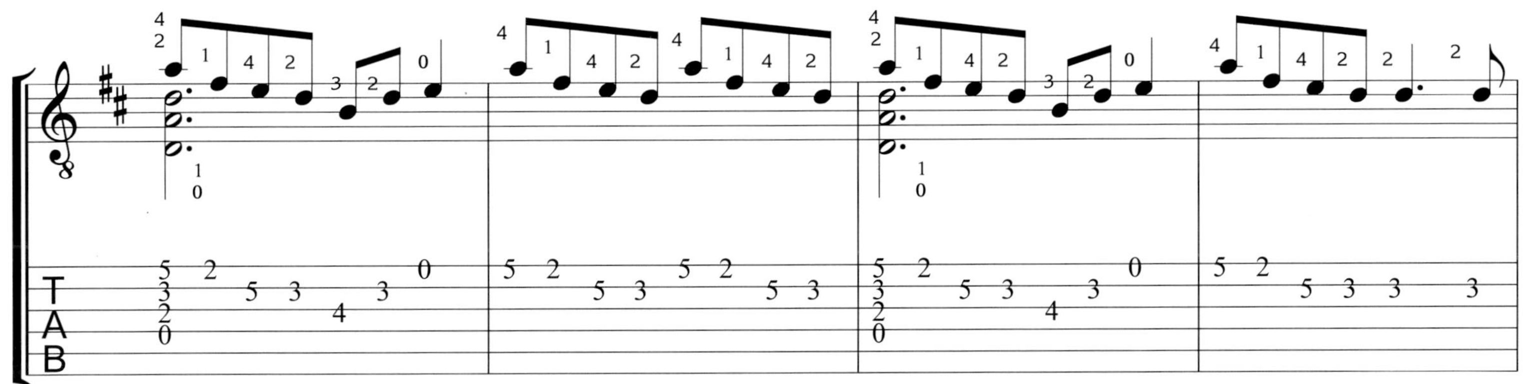

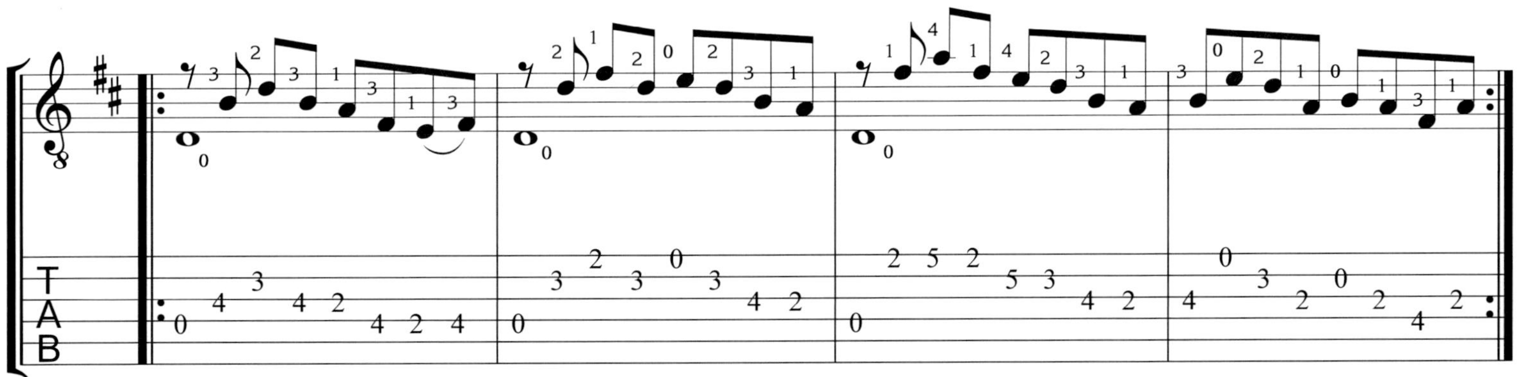

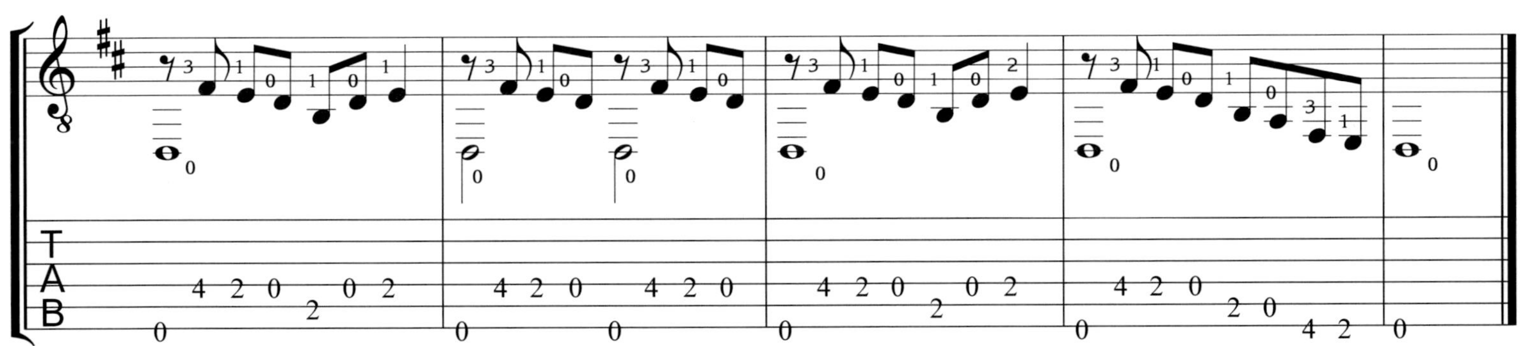

Turlough Carolan

Carolan's Welcome Home

Arrangement by
Allan Alexander

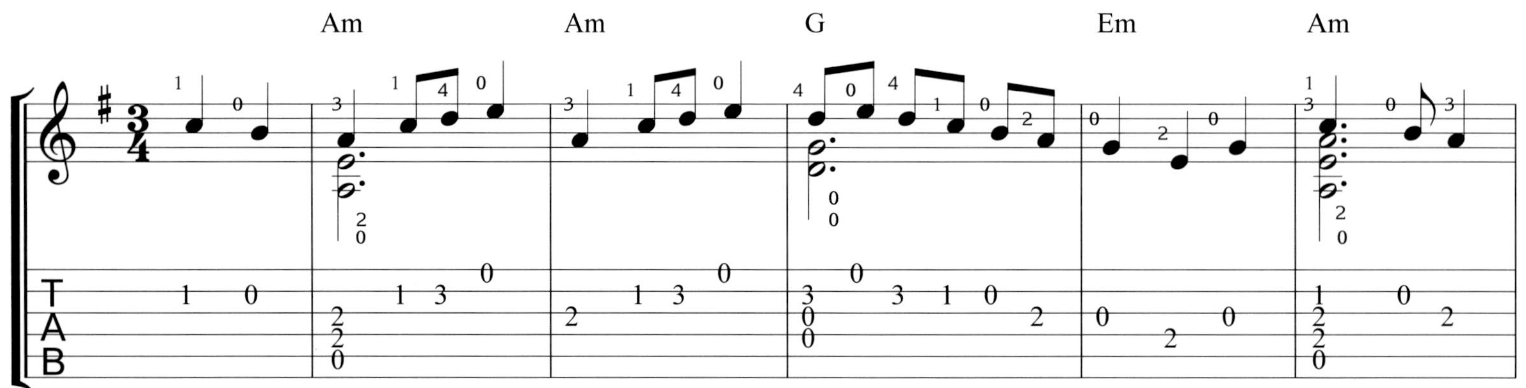

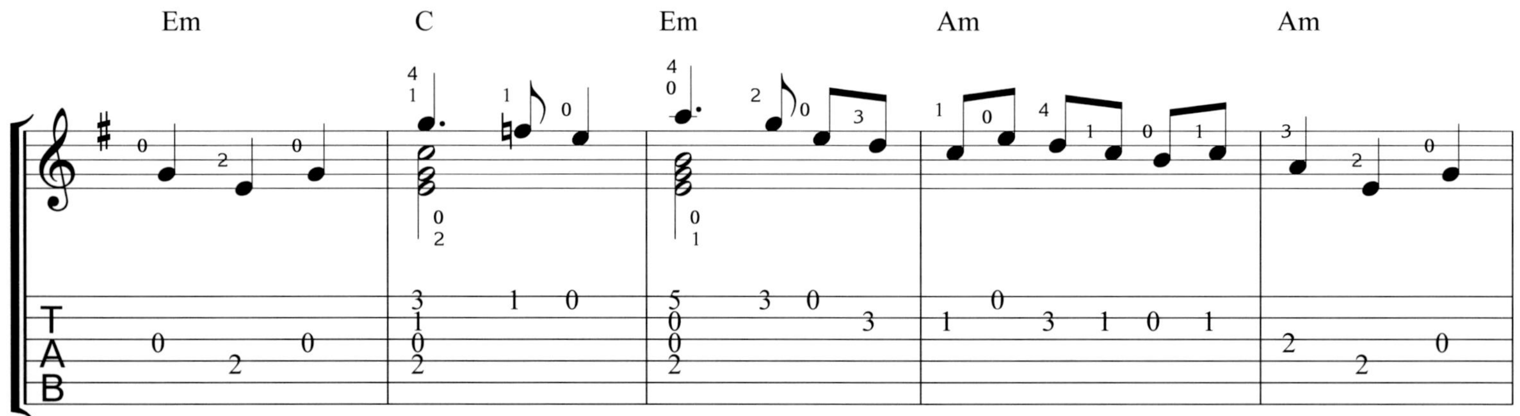

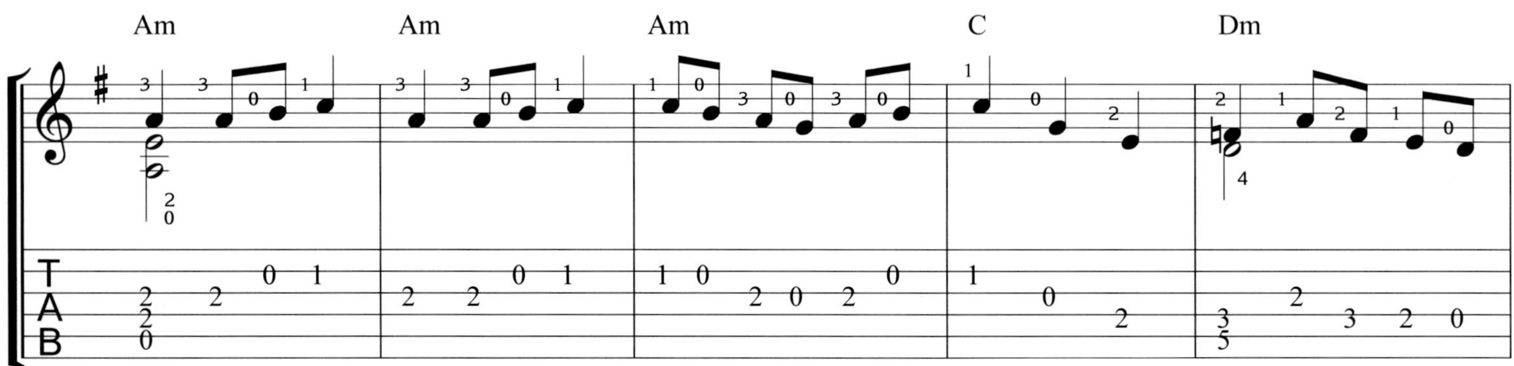

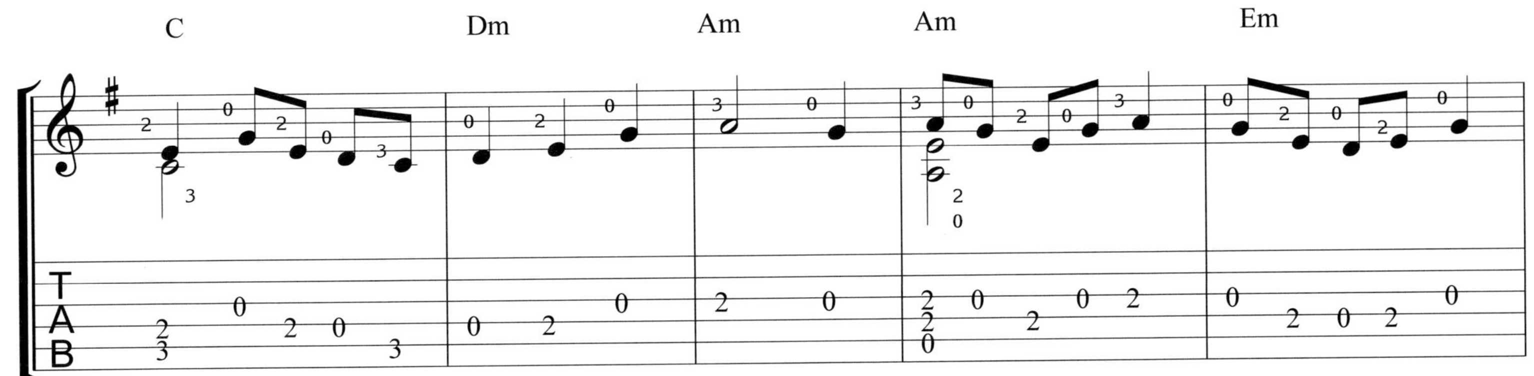
C
Dm
Am
Am
Em
T
A
B

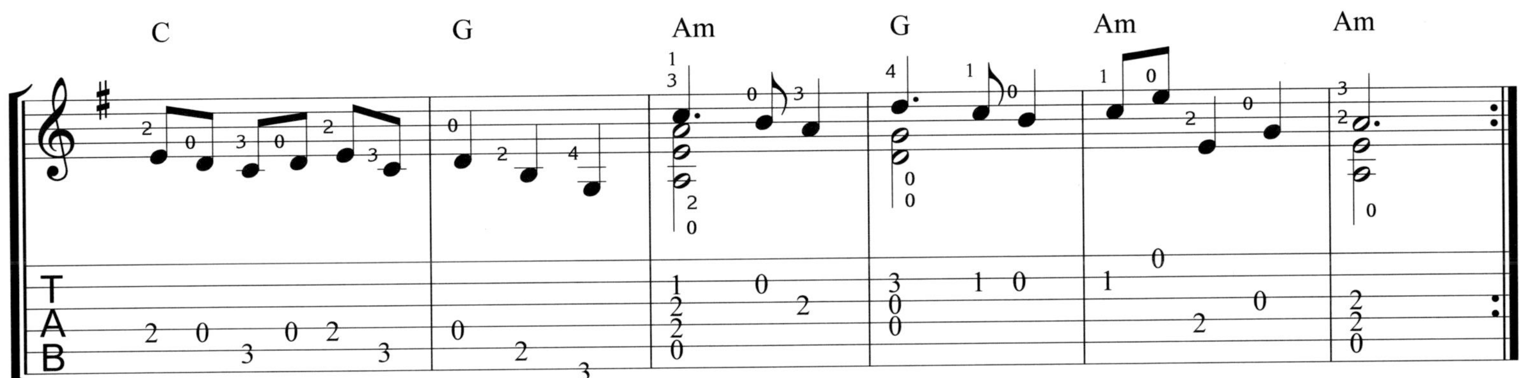
C
G
Am
G
Am
Am
T
A
B

Traditional

Star of the County Down

Setting & Variations by
Allan Alexander

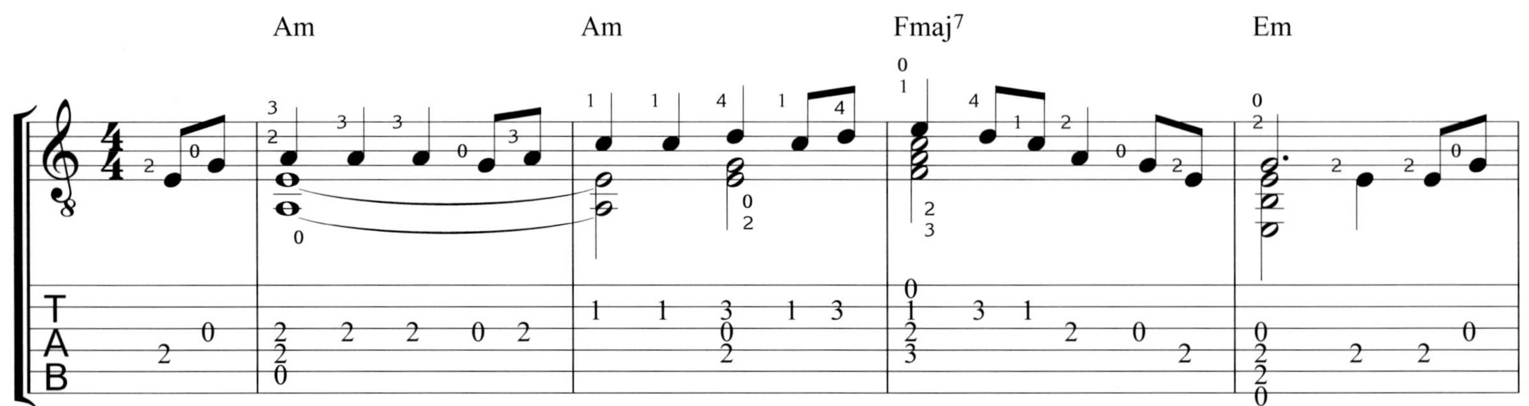

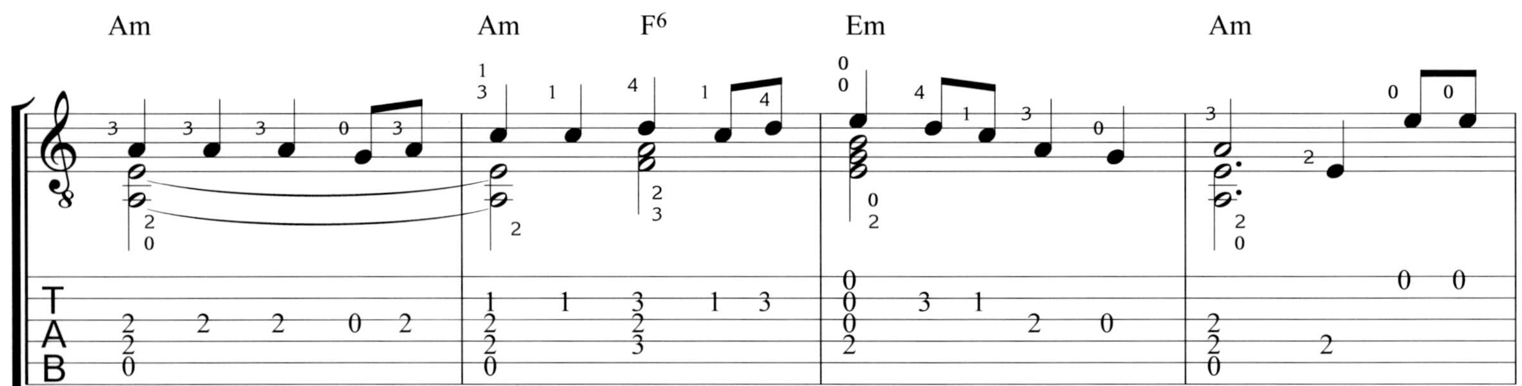

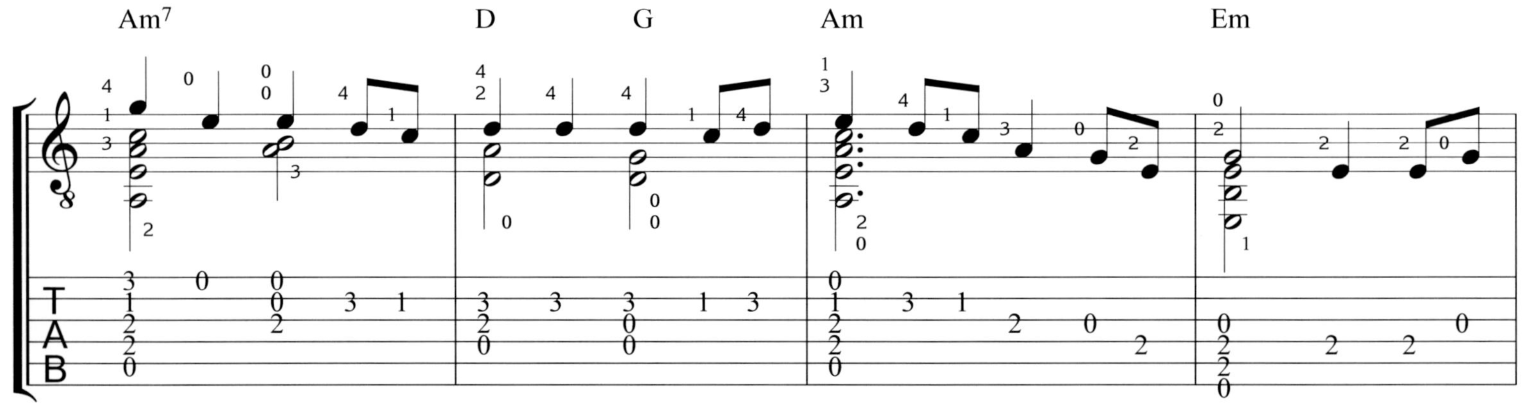

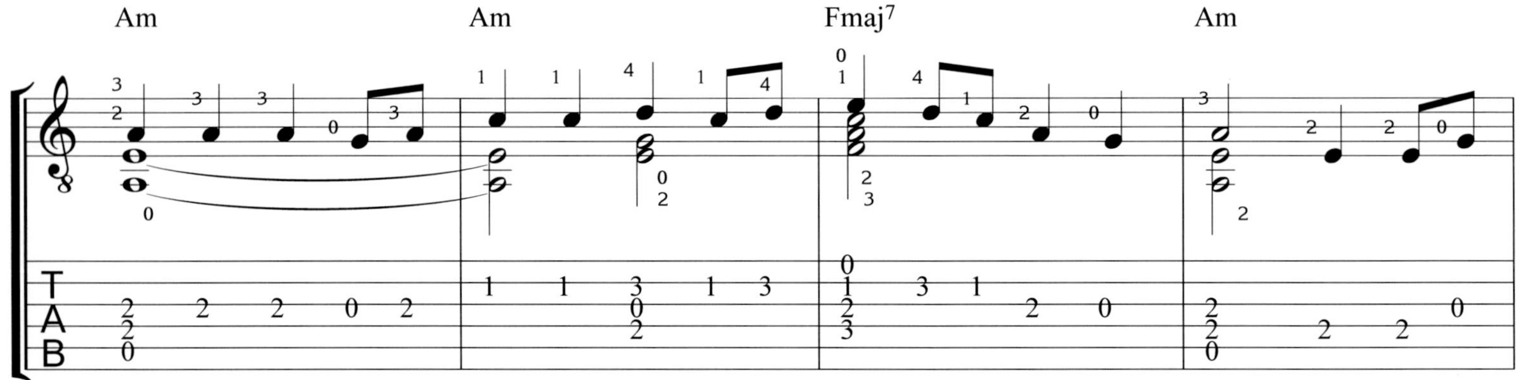

Am
Em
F6
Am
Variation
2/3 BIII

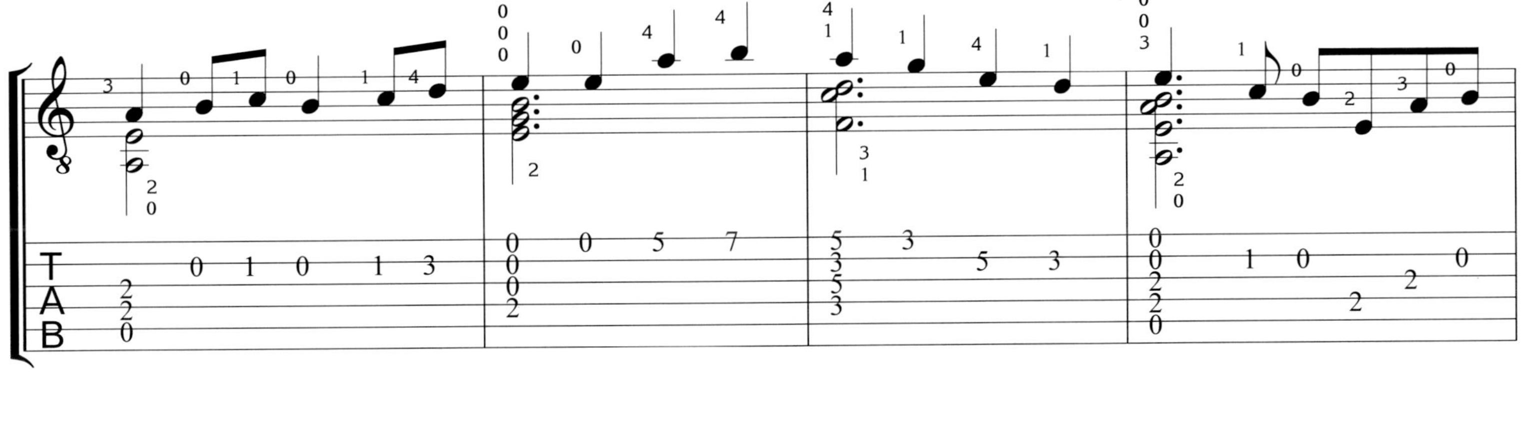
Am
Em
F6
Am
2/3 BIII

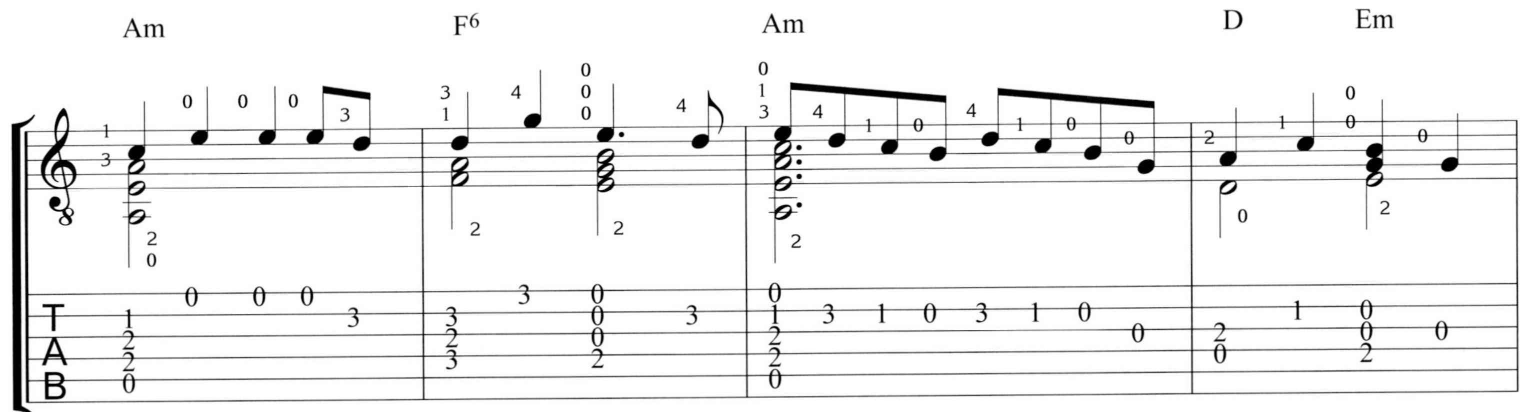
Am
F6
Am
D
Em

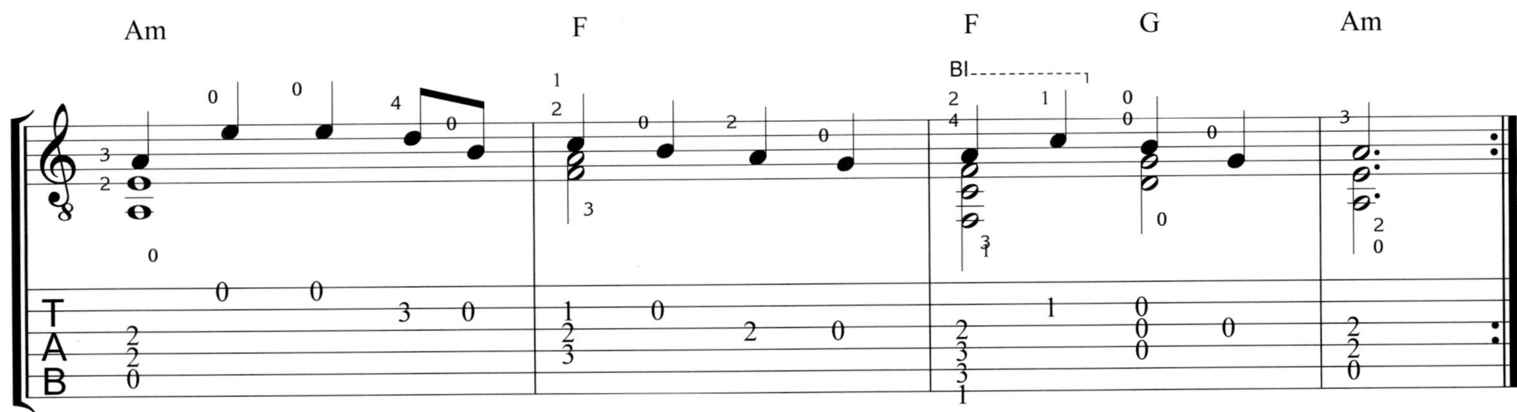
Am
F
F
G
Am
BI

Turlough Carolan

Sheebag Sheemore

Arrangement and Variations
by Allan Alexander

Variation
D
Bm
G
D
G
A
D
Bm
G
D
Gmaj7
Bm
G
F♯m
G
D
D
A
G
D
A
Bm
G
Em
D
Bm
G
D
G
F♯m
G
D
D
1.
2.

Turlough Carolan

The Queen's Dream

Arrangement & Variation by Allan Alexander

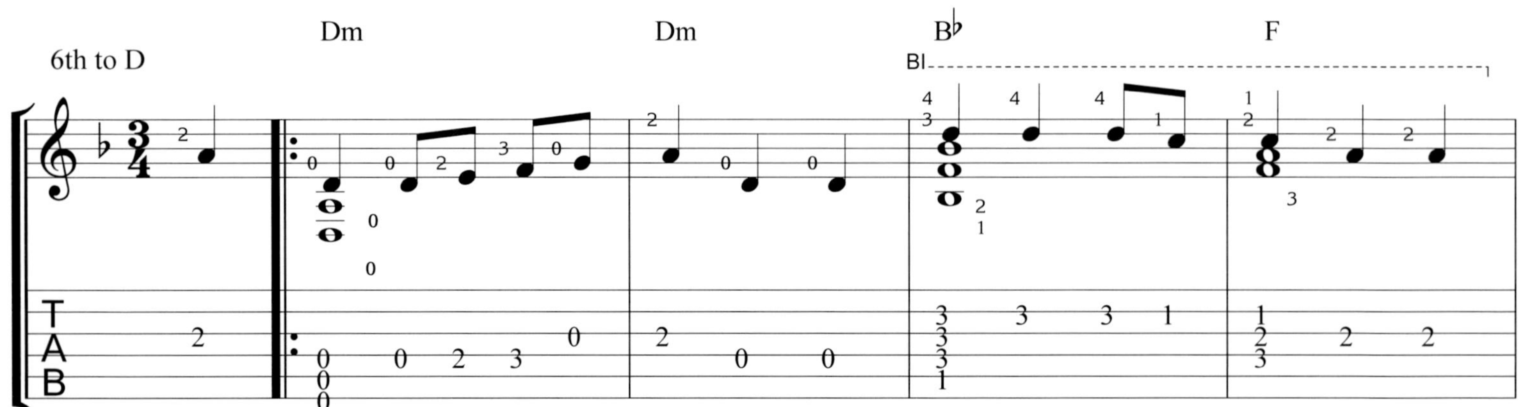

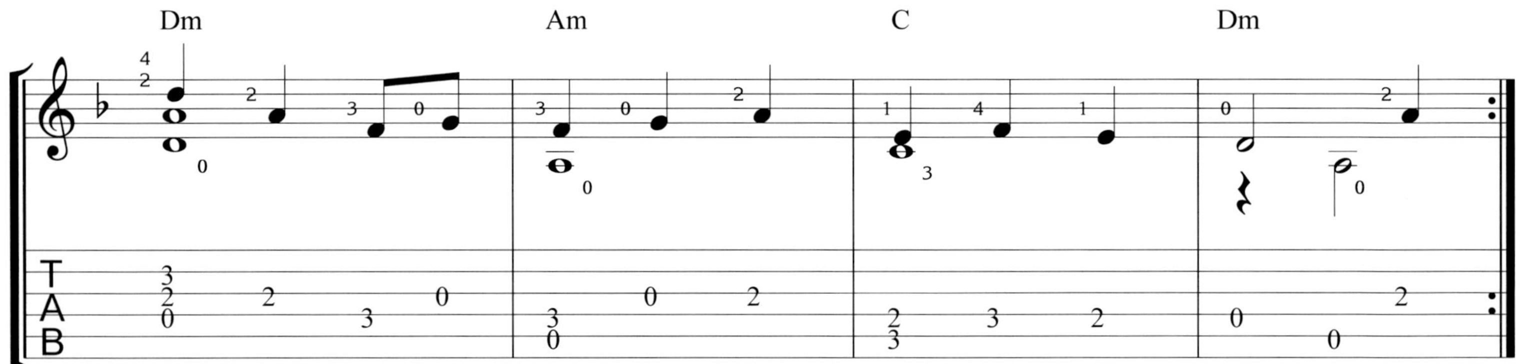

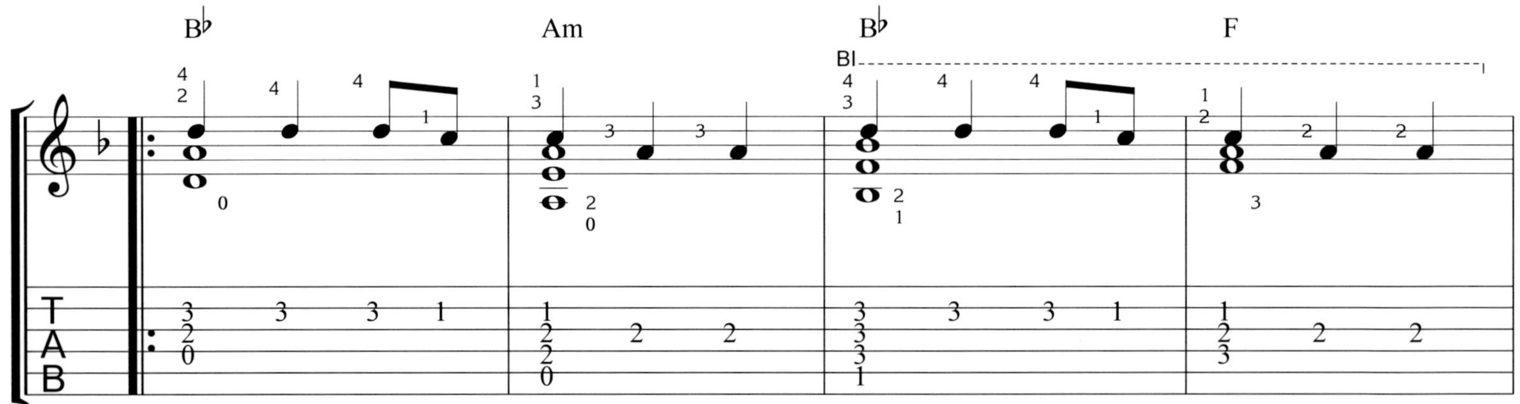

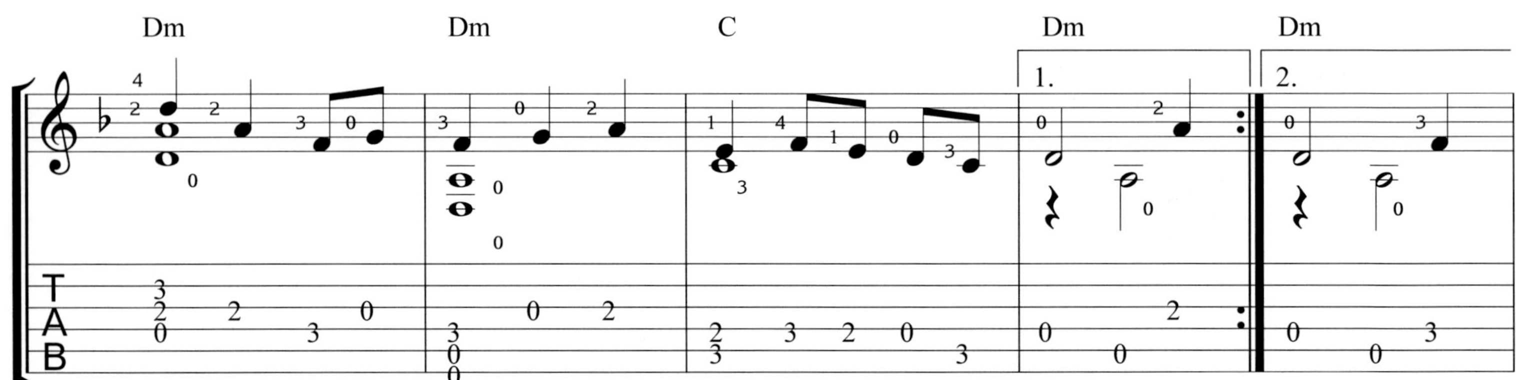

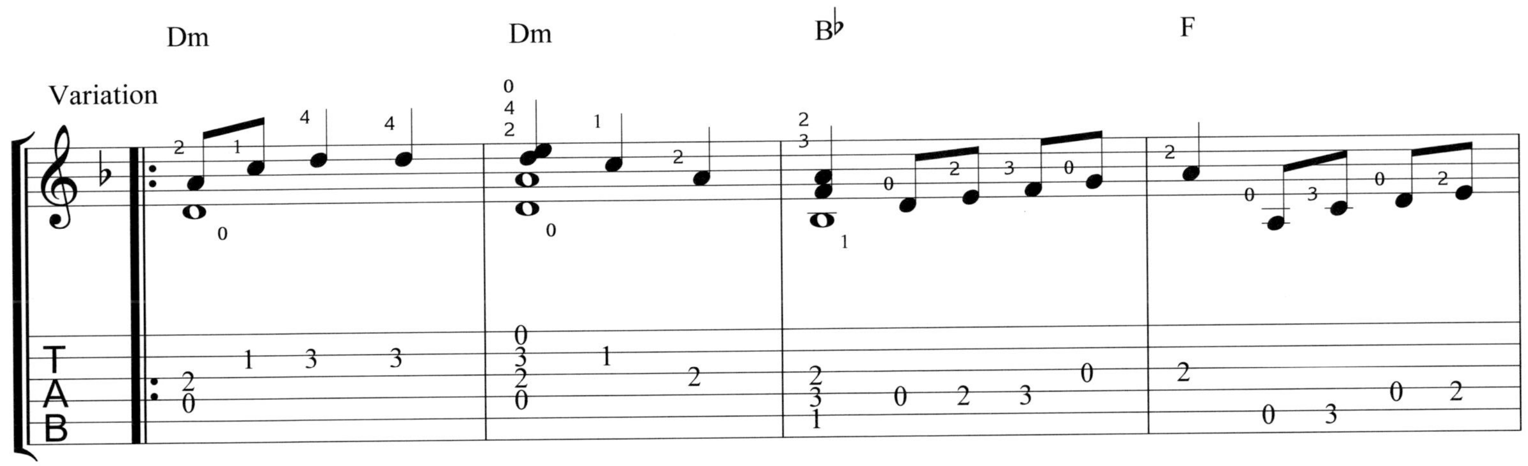
Dm
Dm
B♭
F
Variation

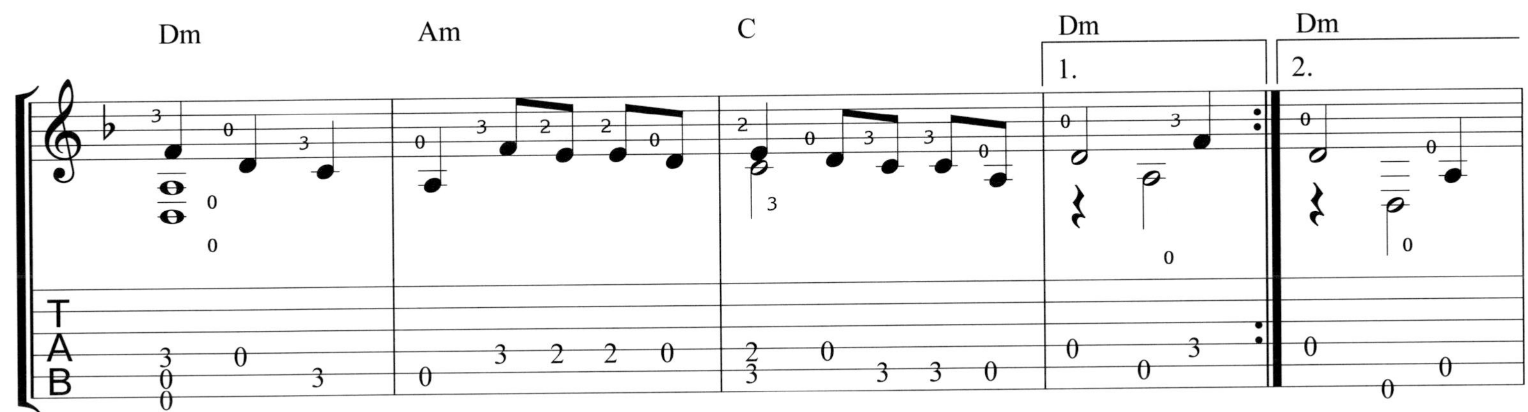
Dm
Am
C
Dm
1.
Dm
2.

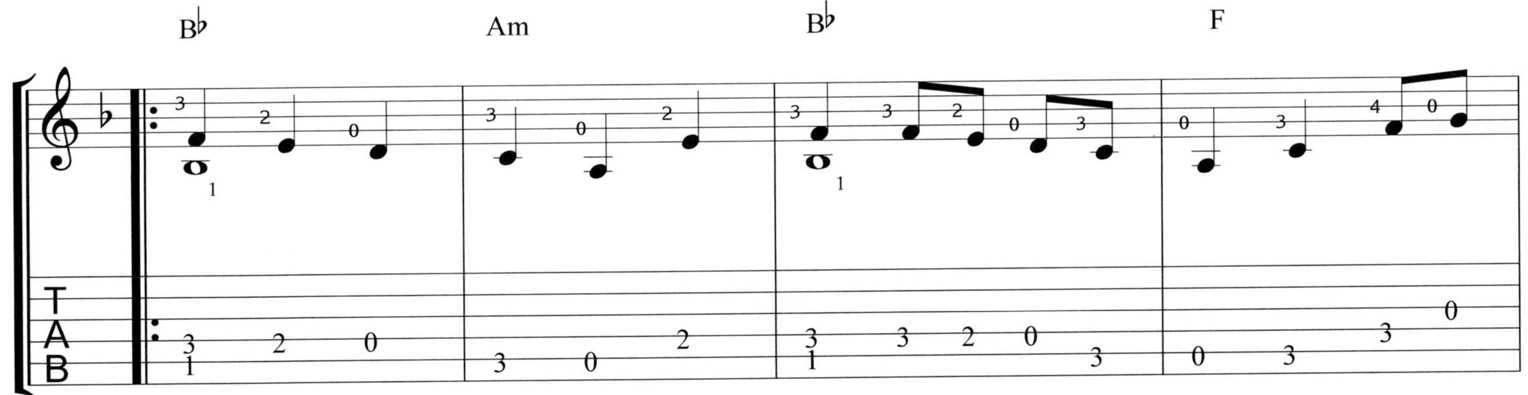
B♭
Am
B♭
F

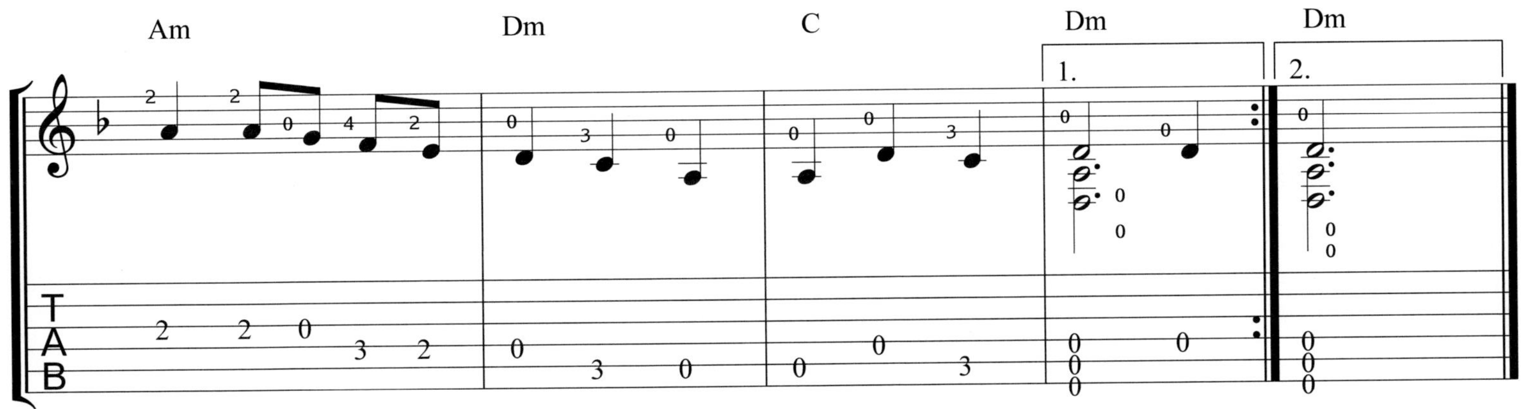
Am
Dm
C
Dm
1.
Dm
2.

Traditional

Nyth Gwcw

Arrangement and Variations
by Allan Alexander

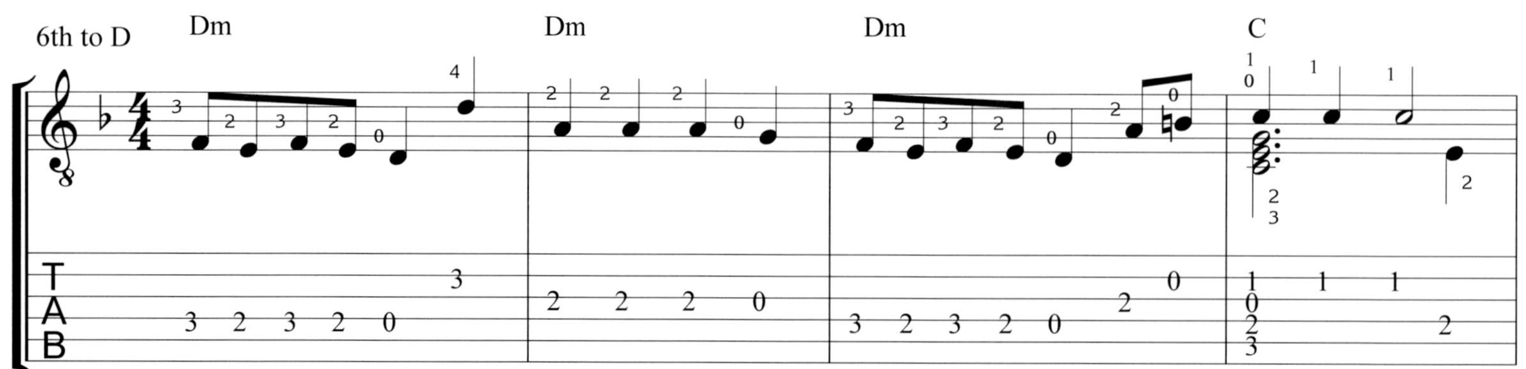

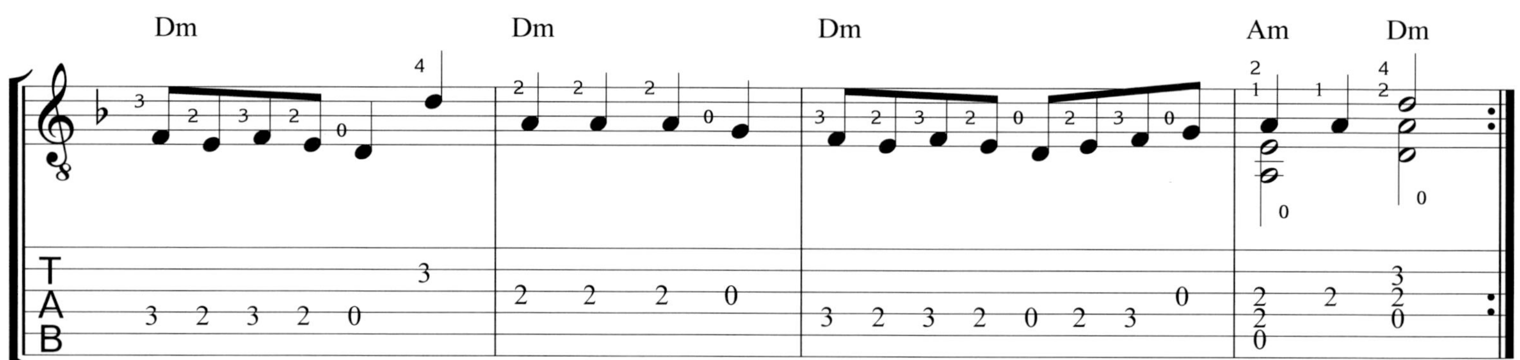

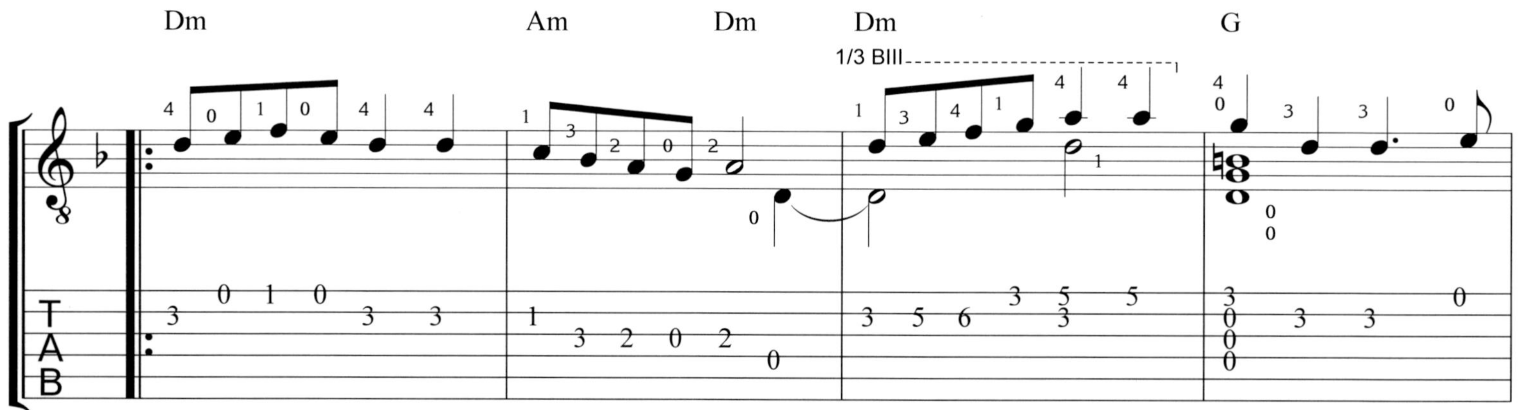

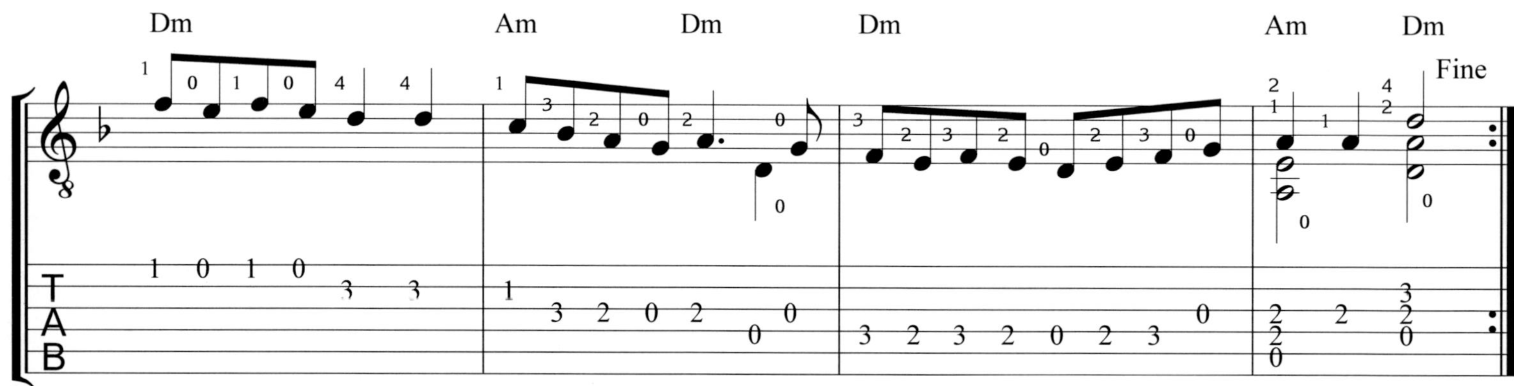

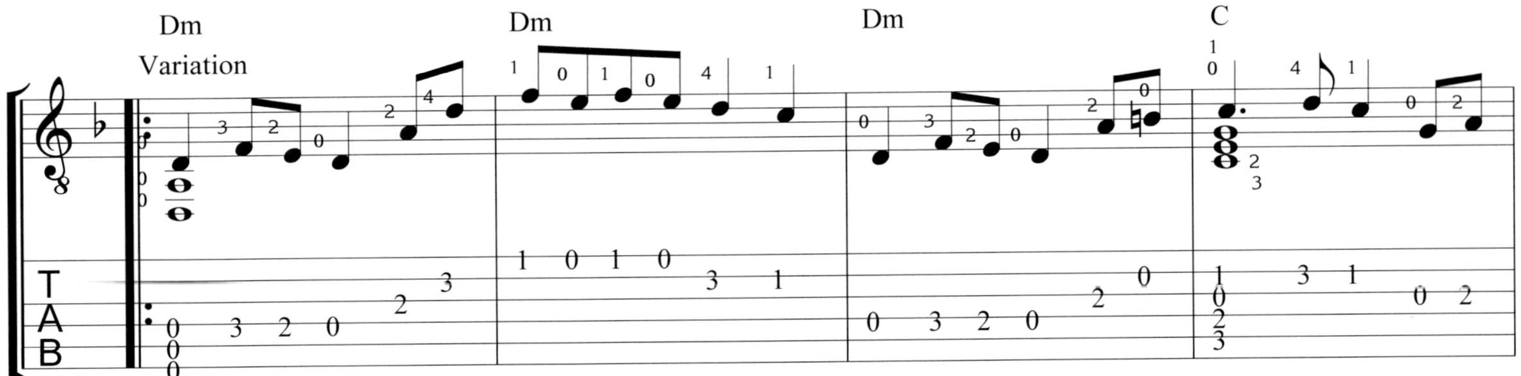
Dm
Variation
Dm
Dm
C
T A B

Dm
Dm
Dm
Am
Dm
T A B

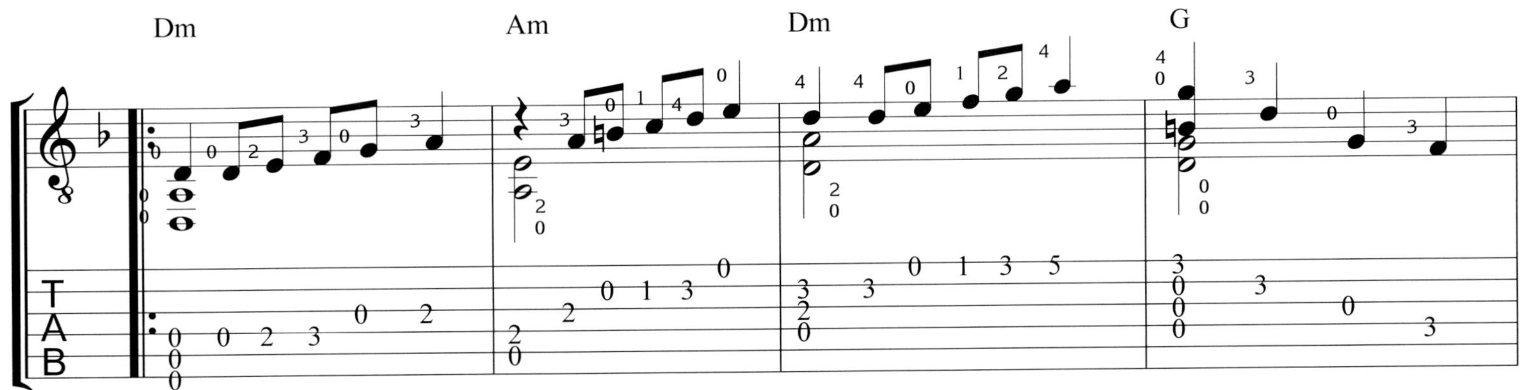
Dm
Am
Dm
G
T A B

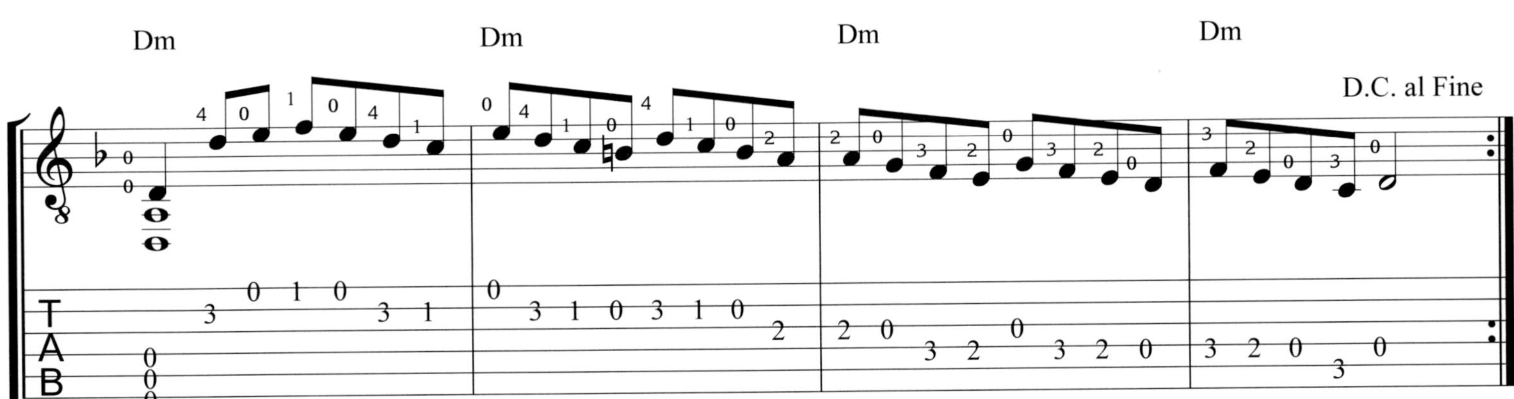
Dm
Dm
Dm
Dm
D.C. al Fine
T A B

Scottish Lute Piece

Lady Laudian's Lilt

Arrangement & Variation by
Allan Alexander

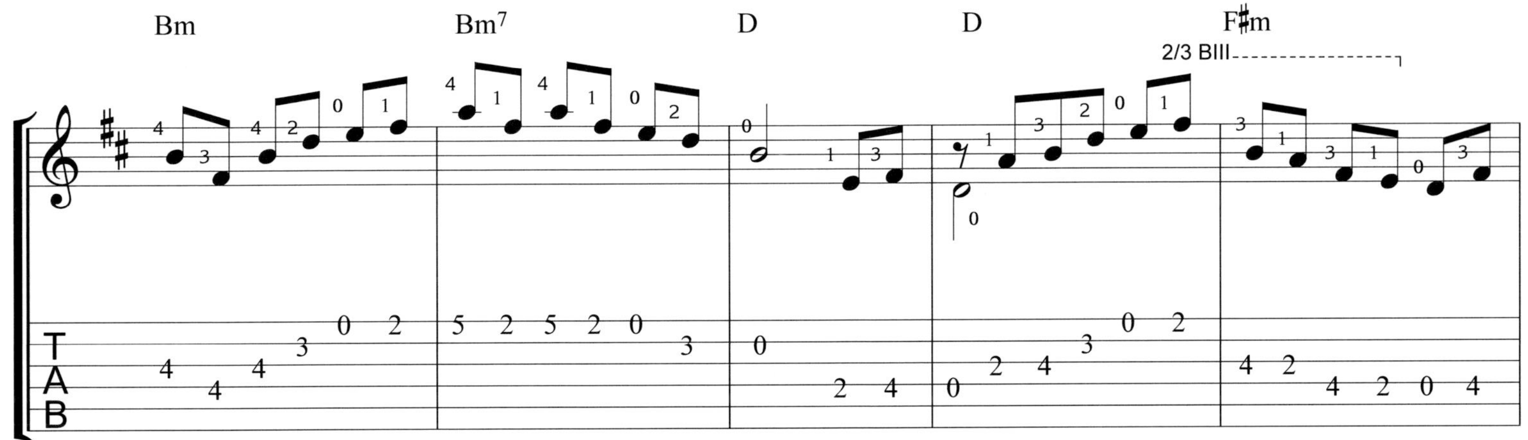
Bm
Bm7
D
D
F♯m
2/3 BIII
T
A
B

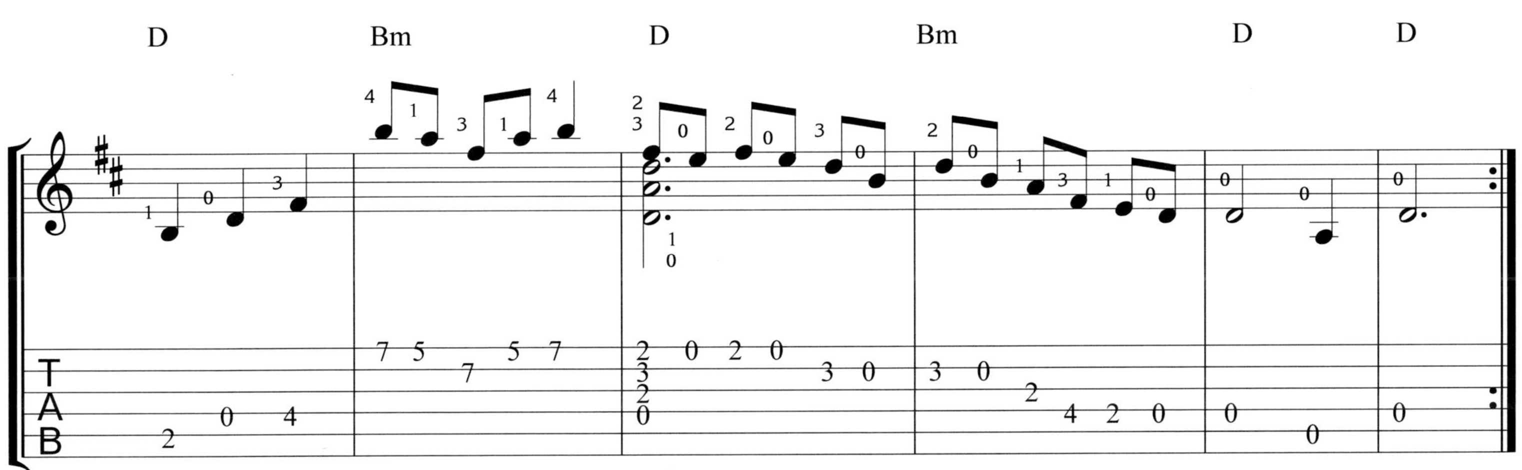
D
Bm
D
Bm
D
D
T
A
B

Turlough Carolan

Fanny Power

Arrangement by
Allan Alexander